D1442366

# CREATING SMALL WOOD OBJECTS
## as Functional Sculpture

*Books by Dona Z. Meilach in Crown's Arts and Crafts Series*

BOX ART: ASSEMBLAGE AND CONSTRUCTION
CONTEMPORARY ART WITH WOOD
CONTEMPORARY BATIK AND TIE-DYE
CONTEMPORARY STONE SCULPTURE
CREATING MODERN FURNITURE
MACRAMÉ ACCESSORIES
MACRAMÉ: CREATIVE DESIGN IN KNOTTING
A MODERN APPROACH TO BASKETRY
PAPIER-MÂCHÉ ARTISTRY
SOFT SCULPTURE AND OTHER SOFT ART FORMS
COLLAGE AND ASSEMBLAGE
    with Elvie Ten Hoor
DIRECT METAL SCULPTURE
    with Donald Seiden
SCULPTURE CASTING
    with Dennis Kowal

*Also*
ACCENT ON CRAFTS
THE ARTIST'S EYE
CONTEMPORARY LEATHER: ART AND ACCESSORIES
CREATING ART FROM FIBERS AND FABRICS
CREATING WITH PLASTER
MAKING CONTEMPORARY RUGS AND WALL HANGINGS
PAPERCRAFT
PRINTMAKING
COLLAGE AND FOUND ART
    with Elvie Ten Hoor
CREATIVE STITCHERY
    with Lee Erlin Snow
HOW TO CREATE YOUR OWN DESIGNS
    with Jay & Bill Hinz
WEAVING OFF LOOM
    with Lee Erlin Snow

*And*
THE ART OF BELLY DANCING
    with Dahlena

# CREATING SMALL WOOD OBJECTS

## as Functional Sculpture

### by DONA Z. MEILACH

Consultant: Lawrence B. Hunter
San Diego State University, California

CROWN PUBLISHERS, INC., NEW YORK

Dedicated to:

My husband . . . Dr. Melvin M. Meilach whose
patience and put-up-with-me ability
during the gathering and writing stages of
a book are beyond the capacity of normal
human endurance.

©1976 by Dona Z. Meilach

All rights reserved. No part of this book may be reproduced or
utilized in any form or by any means, electronic or mechanical,
including photocopying, recording, or by any information
storage or retrieval system, without permission in writing from
the Publisher.

Inquiries should be addressed to Crown Publishers, Inc.,
One Park Avenue, New York, N.Y. 10016.

Printed in the United States of America
Published simultaneously in Canada by
General Publishing Company Limited

Designed by Laurie Zuckerman

APR 6 1979  79-572
Library of Congress Cataloging in Publication Data

Meilach, Dona Z
    Creating small wood objects as functional
sculpture.

    Bibliography: p.
    Includes index.
    1.  Woodwork.  2.  Treenware.  I.  Hunter,
Lawrence B.  II.  Title.
TT180.M38  1976     745.51      75-37531
ISBN 0-517-51866-X
ISBN 0-517-51867-8 pbk.

Fourth Printing, March, 1978

# Contents

Foreword and Acknowledgments        vi

**1** The Heritage of Functional Wood Objects        1

**2** Wood: Its Structure and Physical Properties        23

**3** The Turned Wood Object        43

**4** The Laminated Object        99

**5** The Carved Object        115

**6** Inlay and Marquetry        185

**7** Constructing and Carving        205

Selected Bibliography        238

Wood Associations        242

Sources for Supplies        243

Index        245

# Foreword and Acknowledgments

When I first thought through the idea for *Small Wood Objects*, I visualized a book of about 150 pages—displaying perhaps 200 to 250 examples. As contacts were made with craftsmen, colleges, art schools, and designers throughout the country, the subject exploded into the present volume, with 588 photos. These examples, plus scores more that could not be squeezed in, emphasized the validity of a comprehensive investigation into this little-touched-upon area of contemporary creativity. Even as I was putting the final touches on the manuscript, museums and galleries, aware of my research, were contacting me for craftsmen whose work they could display in exhibits of "small wood objects." Wondrous things happen when an idea meets its time.

And it is certainly time to thank the many people who have contributed their individual experiences. I especially want to express my continuous gratitude to Lawrence B. Hunter, San Diego State University, California, who demonstrated several processes throughout the book and served as all-around consultant. His own examples, which I discovered during research for *Creating Modern Furniture*, were among those that inspired me to delve into small wood objects.

Milon Hutchinson of Capistrano Beach, California, deserves my award for most innovative woodworker. His workshop is a veritable museum of inventive, improvised items for original approaches to the craft. Milon and his wife, Mabel, always dropped whatever they were doing to welcome us, to show us his recent objects, and to share enthusiastically the latest solutions to his woodworking problems.

I loved the week I spent photographing objects in the San Francisco/Berkeley area, thanks to the efforts of William Jaquith Evans. With his superefficiency, he invited local craftsmen to bring their objects to "lunch" at various times during the day. We had set up a photo studio in his living room and proceeded to shoot the wildly marvelous things that were brought in by about fifteen people—many of whom stayed to see what everyone else was doing. The beauty of the experience was that many of the craftsmen knew of one another, but didn't know each other; the day ended with everyone sipping wine and swapping experiences, solutions to problems, markets, where to find sources for woods, and dates to visit at one another's studios. Thanks again, Will, for all your hospitality, including your superb Spanish omelet.

When Mel Morduant, also of Berkeley, offered to demonstrate his wood inlay methods in sleek, beautiful vases, I practically followed him home. His comments after reading the copy are ones I will treasure. I also wish to acknowledge with gratitude, the help of Rudy Hurwich, Berkeley, who drove me through the freeways and byways of Marin County to visit Espenet, J. B. Blunk, John Bauer, and others in the area. To all of them, thanks for their hospitality.

Thanks to Jocko Johnson, Capistrano Beach, California, for the demonstration with the chain saw in chapter 5. It was a revelation to see how rapidly he attacked the raw wood and changed it into a beautiful object.

A fun trip to Tijuana, Mexico, resulted in the demonstration on page 122 by Mexican craftsman José Margaro Quiroz. We had admired the carving of the Muñoz furniture factory; and when Leonard Muñoz invited us to photograph anything we liked for the book, we quickly took advantage.

We enjoyed seeing the work of the professors and students at California State University, Long Beach, California. Our thanks to the woodworking teachers, Frank E. Cummings III and John Snidecor, for your warm welcome, for showing us around, and for contributing your own marvelous examples to the book. The same thanks goes to Tom Tramel, University of California, Northridge.

My sincere appreciation to the northeastern contingent of artists who demonstrated working techniques. William E. Brewerton of Rochester, New York, developed the series on marquetry in chapter 6. His prizewinning examples and easy approach are invaluable assets to the reader.

When Paul S. Kopel wrote about his method of making objects from clay models, interpreted into plastic foam and then into wood laminates, it was too late for me to return to Rochester. Thanks, Sally K. Davidson, for your excellent photographic records of both Bill Brewerton's and Paul Kopel's work.

Thanks, too, to William A. Keyser, School for American Craftsmen, Rochester Institute of Technology, New York, for your tour through the school and for the opportunity to see and photograph the work of your graduate students.

Stephen Hogbin welcomed me to his studio as I passed through Toronto between a workshop and a flight to Rochester. We photographed his pieces, and then both drove to the airport for trips to different destinations. Thanks, too, Steve, for sharing the drawing of your unique lathe with our readers.

I especially want to tell Barbara and Wayne Chapman of Solana Beach, California, how great I think they are. They opened their fantastic collection of art objects and permitted us to photograph anything we wanted. I was particularly eager to show historical examples that had not been seen in other books. Their selective eye and appreciation of the unusual resulted in the many objects shown that help make the insight into the history of the craft so rich. .

Of course, I am indebted to the individual craftsmen who corresponded with me, who took and retook photos until they were usable, and to those who shipped their work for me to photograph. Without this response and cooperation from craftsmen everywhere, the book would not be possible.

I must mention, with gratitude, the very helpful industrial sources: Edelstaal of Tenafly, New Jersey; Dremel Manufacturing Company, Racine, Wisconsin; and Merit Abrasive Products Company, Compton, California.

My thanks to my typist, Marilyn Regula, Morton Grove, Illinois, for her usual incredible analysis of my rough drafts. Thanks to Astra Photo Service, Inc., Chicago, and to Visual Productions, San Diego, for your part in processing the photos taken under the most variable conditions possible.

As always, and above all, I wish to thank my husband, Dr. Melvin Meilach, for his aid and encouragement throughout the long gathering and creative process of a book. And for his acceptance of "women's lib" long before it became a national phenomenon. And to my editor, Brandt Aymar, who has been enduring my writing ups and downs almost as long as my husband has. His luck is that he does it long distance.

Artists whose work appears in the book may be contacted for commissions or exhibitions. Direct your inquiry to the author c/o Crown Publishers, One Park Avenue, New York, N.Y. 10016.

DONA Z. MEILACH

*All photos not otherwise credited are by Dona and Mel Meilach.*

*Above:* Bowls by Bob Stocksdale are lathe turned, subtly shaped. *Clockwise:* Footed bowl of cocobolo, 3 1/4'' high, 6 1/4'' diameter. Salad bowl of English walnut, 4 1/2'' high, 10 1/4'' diameter. Bowl of lignum vitae, 3 1/4'' high, 4'' diameter.

*Opposite:* By Melvin Lindquist, turned burl vase, spalted yellow birch, 5'' high, 3 3/4'' diameter.

*Photo, Bob LaPree*

# The Heritage of Functional Wood Objects

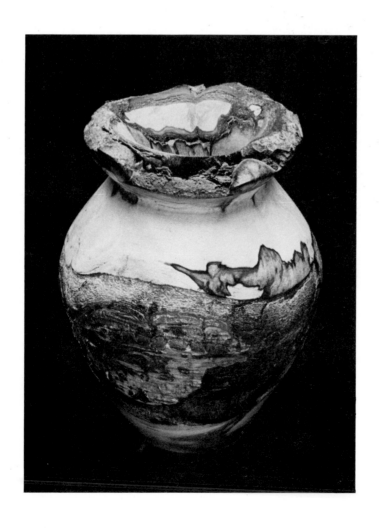

Functional wood objects have probably existed from the beginning of man's first involvement with carving wood, probably since the dawn of civilization all over the world. In Egypt, the carpenter's craft, somewhat hampered by the scarcity of good timber, was far advanced in the early dynastic period. Extant fragments indicate that in the Middle Kingdom, and more particularly during the eighteenth and nineteenth dynasties (1570-1200 B.C.), cabinetmaking attained a new excellence. Chairs, chests, and other articles of furniture were often elaborately decorated with veneer, inlay, and marquetry—all techniques still widely used today. On a smaller scale, delightful trinket boxes, cosmetic spoons and other toilet articles, gaming pieces, handles of sticks and whips were exquisitely carved in both wood and ivory and delicately painted and inlaid.

There are examples of carved wood bowls from the early Oriental cultures dating back as far as the end of the Chou period around 300 B.C., their heavy lacquer finishes evidently preserved them from the ravages of moisture and age. Because of the nature of wood, and its tendency to deterioration in moist climates, early examples are not nearly as prevalent as work in stone, ceramics, and other more stable media.

The most obvious examples of early wood objects are religious items used by many cultures and especially those that date from very early times in India, Egypt, and the Orient. One wonders whether statues of Buddha should be classed as "sculpture" or as "functional objects." But it really doesn't matter. One can safely assume that if wood was used and carvers existed, there also were myriad objects made for everyday purposes to which little value was attached by collectors until fairly recent times. Such items undoubtedly included bowls made from pieces of log for mixing grains, pipes for smoking, toys for children and for adult ceremonies, musical instruments, and household items.

*Above:* A Japanese *chasen*, translated as a "tea whisk," is handcarved from one piece of 5/8-inch-diameter bamboo only 4 1/2" high. Making a *chasen*, used for whipping the tea during the tea ceremony, is a highly skilled technique. It involves dipping the bamboo in hot water for a few seconds then making progressively thinner splits radially until there are about 120 divisions.

*Collection, author*

*Right:* A *wayang golek*, hand-carved puppet head used by a troupe of traveling players. Bali. 14" high, 8" diameter.

*Collection, Mr. and Mrs. W. Chapman*
*Solana Beach, California*

*Opposite:* Wooden box with carved decoration, on one end, representing a human face, bird figures and animals on other sides. Haida Indians, Queen Charlotte Island, Alaska, about 1850—1857.

*Courtesy, Museum of the American Indian,*
*Heye Foundation, New York*

One of the problems in analyzing wood objects historically is the difficulty in stating with certainty the kind of wood used. With so many species and varieties of trees, it would be pure speculation to pinpoint the origin of a bowl based on the type of wood used as coming from a specific oceanic island, for example. Scores of islands would have had similar trees. The same type of tree could easily have existed in other parts of the world at the same time or centuries later. There are no signatures or dates as in sculpture, no hallmarks as in silver. Also, only speculation can suggest the exact purpose of many objects or why they were made of wood rather than some other material. Even carbon dating is "iffy." It can establish within reasonable limits when a tree died, but not when the objects made from the tree were actually made. Probably the most useful application of carbon dating for wooden objects is found in rock tombs where a date of within a hundred years or so may be established, instead of a guess of one or two thousand years. However, bacterial and fungal growth and other vicissitudes that hit woods can upset calculations.

Thus the early history of functional wood objects must remain vague. We must be content examining objects made by various cultures for design, use, content, technique, and any reason that interests the observer. For our purposes, the richest examples probably are the so-called "primitive" wood objects from African countries.

## AFRICAN OBJECTS

Much has been written about African art since it was first "discovered" in the early 1900s by the French sculpture community. Since then, its variety, decoration, design, and general aspects have provided a marvelous inspirational source. The volumes available have concentrated heavily on ritual figures, furniture, and masks. But there are many other objects one can turn to for an insight into exciting forms that are primitive in conception, yet functional and extremely sculptural. There are carved doors and the hardware on them—locks and hinge devices that are simple yet effective in function and design. Large trees are hollowed out and portions used for drums, grain mortars, beer troughs. There are wooden mortars and pestles, beaters, musical instruments, stools, canes with intricately carved handles, knife sheaths. vases and wooden pots, dishes, plates and cups, weaving bobbins, heddles, fetish figures, headrests, combs, arm and ankle bracelets, pipes—the list is endless.

The African carvers' use of wood is fascinating; one reason is its availability, but the social and religious conceptions are of intrinsic importance. To the African, spirits reside in the wood of the tree, even after it is cut down. The fear of forces unleashed by working the material requires a compliance with certain rules before the wood can be carved. Therefore to the African, wood is not dead matter but remains a living thing through the entire process. Cutting and chopping wood causes it pain, and the spirit in the tree is begged for forgiveness. There are many different rites in connection with the carving of wood. Before the tree is felled, sacrifices of eggs, fowl, and sheep have to be made.

The African carver holds a high status in the community because he creates very important religious pieces. He is a highly trained craftsman who understands the characteristics of wood, use of tools, and the tribal symbolism. He has been imbued with spiritual and poetic themes and a knowledge of religious ceremony and folklore. Despite the fact that he may be carving sculptures and objects that are traditional and similar to hundreds of others, he strives and achieves a personal identity.

The kind of wood the African carver uses determines the method of working; in the Sudan, carvers work with hardwood to obtain a fairly rough

Bowl with stylized animals and birds from Ch'ang
Sha. Chinese, Chou dynasty, third century B.C.
Red and black lacquer on wood. 2 1/2" high,
10" diameter.
*Collection Seattle Art Museum, Washington*

angular surface; the Baule have a predilection for various kinds of softwoods which they smooth and polish with affectionate care. The most frequently used woods are those from the bombax tree and some that are similar to ebony and mahogany.

The carver works without a vise, using mainly an adz, a small ax with an arched blade at right angles to the handle (see page 35). He holds it by the blade and wields it like a knife with great dexterity, using it to bring out even the finest details. The finishing touches are added with a knife, graving tool, and chisel. For boring holes, he uses a piece of red-hot iron. If rough edges are to be smoothed, the surface is planed and polished with stone splinters, abrasive leaves, or a type of primitive plane. Then the green wood must be protected from weathering and from termites. The artist may polish the wood with a mixture of soot and grease, or put the object into a mud bath for a few days. He may treat the wood with sap from roots and leaves, or with fine camwood powder. The object is then blackened with soot and dust from the hut, worn down by handling, and given a libation of beer and sacrificial blood to bring about the unique bronze-colored patina often seen.

It is interesting to note that the wood items are almost always made out of a single piece of wood so that the form of the tree remains tangible and recognizable. Rarely are two pieces of wood joined by hinging or joinery methods.

## OCEANIC OBJECTS

Oceanic art, too, offers a lush heritage for the carved functional object which is always classed as "sculpture" by authorities. The function is often secondary to its sculptural form, possibly because the Western researcher is not always sure of the function. For the oceanic islanders, many things are influenced and determined by their religion which, to the outsider, seems to have scarcely any apparent connection with the object. For example, spears, in the northern Solomon Islands, are carved with small squatting figures rubbed with lime. They often are so simplified that they seem purely ornamental. Yet the natives believe that without those figures, which they awaken to life by rubbing before a war campaign, the spear would never strike

*Above:* Wood gong for a Buddhist ceremony is made of hardwood, 6" high, 5" wide, 4" deep. When hit with a padded leather-covered hammer, a resonant sound results. The gongs are made in a variety of sizes to yield different pitches.

*Collection, author*

*Right*: Chocolate whips from Mexico are first turned on a lathe. Circles of wood are left around the piece, but unattached, so they twirl. Then each section is hand carved and some areas stained. 12" high, 2" diameter.

*Collection, author*

*Opposite:* Hand-carved bowl from New Guinea illustrates a primitive, yet highly stylized, portrayal of an animal figure.

*Collection, Mr. and Mrs. W. Chapman*
*Solana Beach, California*

its mark. Animal figures on oars or eating utensils commonly have magical functions and are not merely decorative. Other utilitarian objects with magnificent carved forms include hangers, drums, heddles, vessels, dance staffs, canes, and masks.

Oceanic peoples did not have metals with which to work until much later than other cultures, so that for rough work on wood a curved ax with a horizontally set stone blade was used. Finer work was done with knife-sharp sharks' teeth, shell splinters, drills with sea-urchin spines, files made of shark's or ray's skin, or at times with bits of obsidian and other natural materials.

As in the African and many other primitive cultures, the carver was an important person, at least at the time the work was done. In Oceania, as elsewhere, the artist's name was soon forgotten; what mattered was only the religious significance of the object.

Some contemporary primitive societies suggest a slow change in this attitude. A recent exhibition of contemporary African art at the Field Museum of Natural History, Chicago, emphasized the reputation of certain artists whose individual styles in their cultures were as well known as our Western artists are to us.

## JAPAN

One can dip into almost every culture, past as well as present, to find impressive examples of small wood objects. A favorite is the Japanese *netsuke*, a carved toggle of wood, or sometimes ivory, fastened to the end of the cord binding of an *inro*, which is a small composite lacquered wood container for carrying medicines at one's belt. The netsuke was popular for about three hundred years because the Japanese kimono had no pockets. It progressed from a simple container through stages of shaping, carving, and decorating into an object of show and vanity just like rings and other jewelry. The Japanese respect for the craftsman was high, and about half of these small objects were signed by the artist. As the Japanese adopted Western dress with pockets, the netsuke was no longer made.

Ethiopian headrests vary in design and amount of surface decoration. *Above:* A very simple shape with gently curved legs. 9″ high, 8″ wide, 3″ deep. *Right:* A geometrically hand-carved base. 7″ high, 7″ diameter.

*All objects this page:*
*Collection, Mr. and Mrs. W. Chapman*
*Solana Beach, California*

*Above:* A stamp box from India is intricately carved with open surface patterns. 3 1/2″ high, 2″ diameter.

*Opposite:* Carved wooden ball-head Indian war club collected in 1850 from Upper Michigan. 6 1/2″ high, 25″ long.

*Courtesy, Museum of the American Indian, Heye Foundation, New York*

*Above:* A *netsuke* and *inro* from Japan are among the country's finest woodcraft items. The *netsuke* is a carved toggle, fastened to the end of the cord binding of an *inro*, which is a small composite lacquered wood container for carrying medicines at one's belt. This *inro* separates into four separate compartments (seen here separated). When all compartments are closed, it appears as a precious box with a carved landscape.

## INDONESIA

Another favorite object is the *wayang golek*, a painted and dressed three-dimensional puppet, carved of wood and used by the Javanese in their shadow plays. The construction of a golek puppet is as simple as it is ingenious. The principal wooden components are: a roughly shaped truncated torso with a vertical hole drilled through its center; arms in two parts, strung together at the elbow and dangling loosely from the shoulders; a carefully carved and painted head, complete with headdress, and a somewhat elongated neck; and finally, one pointed central rod that serves also as a handle, and two thinner rods attached to the hands. The central rod, which passes through the torso, emerges between the shoulders and serves as a pivot for the head and neck. By twisting the central rod, the puppeteer can make a golek's head turn in all directions and accompany the movements with arm gestures produced by moving the rods attached to the hands.

## EARLY AMERICA

Among recent popular collectibles is the carved wooden toy from early America, even as recent as those made twenty to forty years ago before the advent of the plastics industry. Our romance with nostalgia now permits us to classify some of the windup and pull toys used by children of the past few generations as "art." And the heritage for that is ancient, too. For hundreds of years, movable toys were used to entertain the nobility of many cultures; in fact, toys dating from ancient Egyptian times were manipulated and had movable parts. These are probably the earliest precursors of robotlike creatures that appeared on the drawing boards in the eighteenth and nineteenth centuries during the automation that developed in the Industrial Revolution.

The practice of whittling cannot be ignored in any reference to a background for small wood objects. The items created by working wood with a small penknife had a wide range of uses and certainly were sculptural. Consider the pipes with intricately carved faces, tobacco tamps, whistles, toys and dolls, cane heads, utensils, hair ornaments, thimbles, and other sewing and needlework items.

## FOLK ART

Folk art is abundant in every culture, and small wood objects are evident in a variety of forms. In folk society, there is no distinction between fine and useful arts. Often, because of their isolation from the mainstream of advanced culture, the people must produce their own necessities, thus making all folk art utilitarian. Decoration of useful articles usually arises from simple aesthetic concerns and has no connection with magic or ritual. The surprising resemblance of folk art among works of people widely separated is probably the result of a universality of materials and basic techniques and a similarity of needs.

## TREEN

One author has undertaken the task of chronicling a history of woodware of European origin including articles made in or exported from Europe to the United States, Canada, Australia, New Zealand, South Africa, and other countries where culture derived from Europe. Edward R. Pinto's three

A pair of antelope headpieces used by the Bambara tribe, Mali, Africa, for the Tchi W'ara ceremony. The carved pieces are attached to woven grass caps and worn on the head during a ceremonial dance in honor of the cultivation of corn. Male 38 3/4'' high; female 31 1/4'' high.

*Courtesy, The Art Institute of Chicago*

Helmet mask from the Senufo tribe on the
Ivory Coast of Africa. Called "fire spitter
masks," they are used in rituals to drive
away soul-eaters. The animal forms are
often grotesque and highly imaginative.
40" long.
*Courtesy, The Art Institute of Chicago*

Bambara mask, Mali, Africa, combines carved wood with a metal fore-
head and cheek covering that has
been indented. 13" high, 5 1/2"
wide, 5" deep.
*Collection, Peter Boiger, Oakland,*
*California*

Horned mask, Africa, Bapende culture,
polychromed wood and raffia. 23" high,
11" wide, 9" deep.
*Collection, La Jolla Museum of*
*Contemporary Art, California*
*Gift of Mr. and Mrs. Huston Noyes*

Headdress of the Simo Society, Baga tribe, Guinea. The intricately carved headpiece fits over the dancer's shoulders and is worn during fertility ceremonies.

*Courtesy, The Art Institute of Chicago*

Benin altar head, African culture, wood. 20 1/2" high, 9" wide, 10" diameter.

*Collection, La Jolla Museum of
Contemporary Art Collection,
Mr. Athur Bart, California*

books (see bibliography) discuss the kinds of objects made, their uses when known, and some social commentary about the times and the reasons for the object to have been made. Many of the small wood objects he deals with date from the seventeenth century. His discussion of "treen" is fascinating. *Treen* is defined in the *Oxford Dictionary* as "(i) made of 'tree'; wooden (ii) of or belonging to, obtained or made from a tree or trees—1670."

The *Encyclopaedia Britannica* states that "throughout the Middle Ages wood carving adorned every kind of church furnishing—benches, choir stalls, rood screens, altarpieces, font covers, pulpits, and lecterns—and was also employed in the decoration of small domestic articles (now known collectively as treen), including cups, spoons, molds, nutcrackers, candlesticks, boxes, pipe cases, and many others."

Mr. Pinto notes that references to treen are numerous in old English literature, particularly to chalices, cups, bowls, platters, and "services of treen." He believes that never has the term been applied to any object larger than a spinning wheel. "The term 'treen' usually described the miscellanea of small wood objects in daily domestic or farm use and in trades and professions."

Pinto's vast collection of small wood objects allowed him to observe their forms, and he subsequently wrote ". . . the above evaluation of the word 'treen' remains correct except, perhaps, to add that nearly all the objects formerly described as treen were wholly or in part the product of the turner and that most of them were one-piece objects. Where they consisted of more than one piece, the junction was made by turning means such as a lipped bowl and cover, a stem threaded or dowelled and glued into a base, as opposed to the kind of joints used in cabinetry by the carpenter. Objects intended solely for ornament such as carved figures and panels were never described as treen."

The quality of craftsmanship and the forms of the objects varied considerably by country and time. But the type of object was fairly universal among the countries of origin and includes those used in the apothecary shop and on the farm, objects for eating and drinking, items in the kitchen and laundry along with mortars, grinders and graters, costume accessories, sailors' and fishermen's devices, tools, and many more. The list is encyclopedic, particularly in Pinto's title *Treen and Other Wooden Bygones*, and should be studied by everyone interested in the heritage of the small wooden object.

*Top:* A Dogon lock, African culture, wood and metal, with a latch-locking device, has an animal head shaped at the bottom. 15″ high, 16″ wide, 3″ deep.

*Collection, La Jolla Museum
of Contemporary Art, California
Gift of William Brill Foundation*

*Below:* A contemporary hand-carved door latch by J. B. Blunk of California.

*Opposite left:* Chinese joss-stick holder has holes in the top to receive the sticks of burning incense. Drawers below. 10″ high, 6″ wide, 4″ deep.

*Collection, Mr. and Mrs. W. Chapman
Solana Beach, California*

*Opposite right:* Jewelry chest carved from a piece of log by Dennis Morinaka with beautifully hand-modeled drawer fronts. Approximately 15″ high, 15″ wide, 12″ deep.

## CONTEMPORARY TRENDS AND COUNTERPARTS

One of the many fascinating facets in the emergence of a recognizable trend in contemporary craft circles is the application of the word *object* to small utilitarian items of any medium, whether it is ceramic, silver, glass, fiber, or wood. In Edward R. Pinto's first volume, *Treen, or Small Woodware Through the Ages*, the term "small wood object" is used throughout the book, but one feels the word "object" is a synonym for the word "item" and used as a matter of style rather than referring to specifics such as trays, bowls, candlesticks.

By the mid-1950s the use of the word *object* to signify a useful item made by a serious craftsman appeared regularly in the reviews of exhibitions and in feature articles in *Craft Horizons*, the trend-setting publication of the American Crafts Council and the Museum of Contemporary Crafts, New York. The greatest impetus that gave a "handle" to the effervescent activity was an exhibition titled "Objects: U.S.A.," sponsored by the S. C. Johnson Co., Racine, Wisconsin. A subsequent book also titled *Objects: U.S.A.* published in 1970 enabled the craftsman himself to identify his work with a "movement."

Many serious artists who turned to creating one-of-a-kind handmade crafts with unequaled fervor following World War II were no longer anonymous; they were "object makers" with status as artists. The term *handicraft* became pejorative.

A hand-carved comb from Brazil illustrates meticulous craftsmanship and detail. 13'' high, 2 1/4'' wide.
*Collection, Mr. and Mrs. W. Chapman*
*Solana Beach, California*

Combs by Stephen R. Johnson have a contemporary curvilinear shape. Made of padouk and shedua and ranging in sizes from 3'' high, 6'' long, to 3'' high, 10'' long.

A primitive approach to the comb, still retaining a sculptural form, in the work of contemporary African craftsmen. 8'' high, 2'' and 2 1/2'' wide.
*Collection, author*

*Opposite:* Three views of a hand mirror by Frank E. Cummings III. Ebony with bone and brass. Approximately 10'' high, 5'' wide, 2 1/2'' deep. A modern interpretation of the Ashanti fertility doll.

In reality, the idea of making one-of-a-kind, beautifully formed objects by artists began with the art-craft movement that flourished in England during the latter half of the nineteenth century. Its goal was to bring art into the daily life of all social classes, and the guiding figure of the movement was William Morris (1834-1896).

Morris wished to make art part of the life of the community, to encourage the mass of society to "have nothing in your houses that you do not know to be useful, or believe to be beautiful." As he saw it, the traditional role of art had been enjoyed only by the rich and leisured class. The ideas of Morris and his associates, while not necessarily producing the socialistic trends he propounded, did have a profound influence on matters related to applied arts and architecture in Great Britain, and on the continent. From it emerged the Art Nouveau style, an international movement of "new art" which became current in Europe and the United States at the turn of the twentieth century. The use of the sinuous forms were applied to paintings and sculpture, to architecture and "applied arts," which was the name usually reserved for useful items and in direct opposition to "fine" arts. But the glass vases, wood furniture, stairwells, gates, and other applied arts were credited to individuals—they were not anonymous creations. Such names as Louis Tiffany, Victor Horta, and Henry van de Velde are well known for their contributions to the art object at this period. The Arts and Crafts Movement and Art Nouveau established the artist-craftsman in a position of status in a creative society in Europe. It took longer to reach across the ocean.

The influence of the Bauhaus school in Germany was significant to the growth of the artist-craftsman in Europe and, eventually, in the United States. Walter Gropius's organization of the school enabled the student to be trained by a painter, sculptor, and a master craftsman. He was taught to apply the same aesthetic importance to a painting, a chair, a pot, or a building. Bauhaus students were free to work in oil, yarn, ceramics, wood, or metals; and they could create objects sympathetic to the environment. An example of this total concern with design in every aspect of life was in the architecture of Mies van der Rohe and his insistence on designing the furniture for his buildings so that the total effect would be unified.

Eventually, many of these Bauhaus-trained artists emigrated to the United States where they taught at schools such as the Cranbrook Academy of

An African hand-shaped bowl utilizes some of the organic shaping of the tree in keeping with the native's reverence for the wood itself and also contributing to the design. Ebony and sapwood.

*Collection, Mr. and Mrs. W. Chapman*
*Solana Beach, California*

Elm burl salad bowl (*two views*) by Stephen Hogbin. 9″ diameter. Shaping is accomplished by placing the wood burl on a lathe. The beautiful natural mutation is effectively utilized in the design and grain.

*Opposite:* By Jim Traynor. An irregularly shaped, hand-carved walnut bowl shows how an unusual shape can be created from a log slab. 6″ high, 24″ wide, 20″ deep.

Art in Michigan, Alfred University in New York, and the Institute of Design in Chicago. Their philosophy spread. The woodworker, along with the ceramist, the glassblower, the jeweler, and other artists in various craft media voiced, more vociferously than ever, that there is no distinction between the person who produces painting and sculpture and the one who makes "objects." Their education, approach, experiences are the same: the end product is a work of art regardless of the medium used.

Many of the people whose work appears in this book helped raise the consciousness of the public to see the wooden object as a serious work of art. Some have been involved with wood since World War II and were included in the early shows and exhibits reviewed and encouraged by *Craft Horizons.* Some were furniture makers and sculptors who also created useful objects in the sculptural idiom—simply because that was how they wanted to work and the way they envisioned what a piece should look like. One of the earliest advocates of the sculptural/functional object was Wharton Esherick (1887-1970), who leaves a rich legacy of items in the Esherick Museum, Paoli, Pennsylvania. The role of the furniture maker in the history of this activity can be followed in my earlier book *Creating Modern Furniture* (Crown 1975).

Arthur Espenet Carpenter's influence has been far reaching. Following World War II he bought a lathe and began turning bowls and other treen ware. In a few years his bowls were being sold at select stores across the country and were chosen for the Museum of Modern Art's "Good Design Exhibit" in 1950. Carpenter, who uses the name "Espenet" professionally for obvious reasons, slowly taught himself the necessary skills and acquired machinery for making furniture, for which he is best known today. However, the jewelry boxes and small objects he creates "for fun" are magnificently designed with smooth, rounded surfaces and flowing lines.

Among craftsmen and a majority of knowledgeable noncraftsmen, the name of Bob Stocksdale is almost synonymous with the words "turned bowl." Bob also creates trays and platters; all his objects are outstanding for their unity of material, simplicity of form, and technique. The shape, texture, and finish of his objects are determined by the fullest exploitation of the nature of the wood and its grain patterns. He turns his bowls almost paper thin, while still retaining the essence of the form and material.

It is impossible to single out, in this book, all the craftsmen who deserve special recognition—perhaps at another time—but the objects selected for *Creating Small Wood Objects* are among the best examples of the craft as it is practiced today. The ultimate decision for inclusion was based on form, craftsmanship, variety, and use of the material. There is no distinction made between work created by established craftsmen who may also be teachers and by their students. In fact, many teachers insisted that their students submit work, often photographing the objects themselves to meet the standards necessary for presentation. The result is an almost encyclopedic foray into the contemporary wood object, its makers, and how they work.

*Opposite top:* Bob Stocksdale turns a bowl in the well-equipped basement workshop of his home. His bowls are known for their simplicity of design and shape and the full exploitation of the grain patterns in the wood. *At right:* a cocobolo bowl 3 1/4" high, 6 1/4" deep.

*Opposite below:* Arthur Carpenter (Espenet) has evolved and pioneered a variety of new forms in furniture and accessories that are visually and tactically pleasing and that use an economy of materials and stress function. The jewelry box has a pair of drawers set one within the other that slide forward and are held in place by a locking peg on the right side.

# Wood:
# Its Structure and
# Physical Properties

Hand-carved board push by Stephen Harris. 16″ long.

Bow, or frame, saw by Tim Ellsworth. Hickory wood.

*Opposite top:* The craftsman's tool storage is often handmade to custom fit manufactured and hand-shaped tools.

*Photographed at
Stephen Hogbin's studio
Toronto, Canada*

*Opposite below:* Three hand-carved planes by Paul Epp. Pearwood. From top to bottom, widths are 16″, 13″, 8 1/2″.

Learning the vagaries of wood is a never-ending study. A tree has basic structures and physical properties, but because of the vicissitudes of nature, each species of tree differs from another; each tree within a species will have different characteristics. Even the wood within one tree can vary and offer such variety of grain pattern, texture, and color that the chances of two objects designed, shaped, and created the same way being identical in appearance is highly unlikely.

## WOOD STRUCTURE

All wood comes from trees—a perfectly obvious statement. Technology duplicates tree patterns by photographic processes on industrially made finishes, but wood itself is created only by nature. The fibrous nature of wood strongly influences how it is used. Wood is composed mostly of hollow, elongated, spindle-shaped cells that are arranged parallel to each other along the tree trunk. When a tree is cut into lumber, the characteristics of these fibrous cells and their arrangement affects such properties as strength and shrinkage, as well as the grain pattern of the wood.

In the illustration of the sectioned tree at right the basic features can be seen: 1) The outer bark which is divided into the outer, corky dead portion that varies in thickness and texture with different species and with the age of the tree, and 2) the thin, inner living bark, the "phloem" which is the pipeline through which food is passed. 3) The cambium cell layer is the growing part of the trunk which produces new bark and new wood annually. It is in the cambium that growth rings occur during the tree's early and late growing seasons. 4) Sapwood is located next to the cambium and functions primarily as the mechanical transport of water to the leaves. 5) The heartwood is the central supporting layer of the tree. It consists of inactive cells that have been slightly changed both chemically and physically from the cells of the inner sapwood rings. The heartwood varies in color and texture in various species.

## HARDWOOD AND SOFTWOOD

Trees are divided into two classes: *hardwoods*, which have broad leaves, such as oak, walnut, mahogany, cherry, and ebony, and *softwoods or conifers*, which may have scalelike or needlelike leaves, such as pine, fir, hemlock, holly, and all other evergreens. The terms "soft and hard" have no direct reference to the actual softness or hardness of the wood; rather it refers to the type of cells of which the wood is composed.

Softwood is so called because it has a simple structure and is easily sawed, carved, and nailed. Each ring consists of a single type of cell, the *tracheid* or *fiber*. Seen microscopically, it is a long, slender tube, rather square in cross section with a hollow cavity. The walls of the tube are made up of two carbon compounds, the flexible *cellulose* and rigid *lignin*. The cellulose gives the wood its toughness; the lignin gives it its firmness and solidity. The center of the tube holds a small quantity of living tissue or protoplasm, but is essentially a space for transporting sap. As the sap ascends the tree trunk, it is passed from one fiber to another through minute openings known as *pits*. The types of pits found between the tracheids and storage tissues are usually quite distinctive and aid in identification of various species.

Two other features are present in most, though not all, softwoods—rays and resin. Rays run at right angles to the annual rings and radiate out from the center. In softwoods the rays are usually very narrow and scarcely visible, but in hardwoods they are very obvious. Resin is found exclusively in the softwoods. It is formed in tiny canals that exist vertically and horizontally through the wood; they have little effect on the usability of the wood.

Actual wood samples are available from several wood suppliers. Check listings in Sources for Supplies. Some have labels indicating keys for identifying woods.

Wood veneers and identifying keys can be found in source books such as *Hough's Encyclopaedia of American Woods* by E. S. Harrar. It consists of thirteen volumes showing actual veneers of transverse, radial, and tangential cuts. The volumes are available in some libraries.

Hardwoods as a group are more highly evolved than the softwoods; their wood structure shows much greater variation in cell sizes and arrangements. It is these variations that aid in identification. The distinguishing cell type of the hardwoods is the vessel referred to as a *pore* when seen on the cross section of the wood. The individual vessels are relatively short and open at the ends; their diameters vary so that some are visible to the naked eye, others only with a microscope. Pores also vary considerably in arrangement, but two basic types appear; the pores of springwood are distinctly larger than those in summerwood.

The pores of hardwoods result in a closer grain structure than those in softwoods. This close grain characteristic inhibits splinters and chipping, making hardwoods more desirable than softwoods for carving, wearability, grain pattern, color, and texture. Rays are more obvious in hardwoods than in softwoods, often causing splits or checks as the wood dries out.

## GRAIN, TEXTURE, COLOR

The variety of items created in wood attests to its versatility. The woodworker must decide upon the type of wood he wants for a specific project depending upon availability and his plans for working with it.

The grain, texture, and color of a finished piece of wood are primary considerations in selection. The terms *grain* and *texture* and *figure* are frequently used loosely or are misused. *Grain* refers to the direction of the rays or other longitudinal elements. Grain may be straight, spiral, interlocked, wavy, or irregular.

*Texture* refers to the relative size and variation in size of the cells ranging from fine to coarse and often to uneven. Maple, for example, has cells of small diameter, and the wood is referred to as fine textured. Oak has large diameter cells and is coarse textured. Even-textured woods have cell diameters that are very uniform, while uneven textured woods show a distinct variety in cell diameters.

*Figure* is another aspect of grain pattern that is determined by the way the tree grows during different seasons, the part of the tree from which the wood is taken, and the manner in which the wood is sawed.

Oak, walnut, zebrawood, and rosewood are highly grained and figured because they have a rapid summer growth period. Mahogany grows at a more uniform rate so the pattern is more regular. Ebony usually has only grain and no figure.

Unusual appearance of wood such as speckling, mottling, circling, swirling, and so on appear where the tree has grown in crotches or V-like areas, or where the trunk separates into branches. Burls, which are domelike outgrowths from the trunk caused by broken or cut branches or injuries to the tree, are highly figured because the fibers expand, compress, and encircle the area. Knots, caused by branches breaking, often are found within the tree's trunk between and within the rings. All these malformations can be used advantageously by the artist—although frequently interior injuries and growth changes in a log can also be frustrating when a project is contemplated and the unseen checks, rays, or knots interfere with the planned design.

Two kinds of grain are important to the woodworker: end grain and face grain. End grain is the result of a horizontal cut across a log. Portions of the log's rings, heartwood, and sapwood appear. Face grain runs the length of the dressed board and produces the most beautiful patterns.

*Color* of wood results from the presence of infiltrated compounds in the cell walls and cavities. Usually the color is limited to the heartwood and, given the thousands of different species of trees, an incredible color range may be found from the near white of holly to the jet black of ebony. The color of wood may change when it is exposed to light for long periods. In general, lighter woods darken and darker woods become lighter.

The outer bark

The inner bark

The cambium cell layer

Sapwood

Heartwood

How a tree builds a trunk.
*Courtesy, St. Regis Paper Co., N.Y.*

Interestingly, very few trees have distinctive odors with the exception of cedars, rosewoods, and some firs. Usually any odors disappear after the tree has been cut down.

## How cutting the log changes its appearance

Because of the way that wood is built up, it never appears the same on different cut surfaces. The way the log is cut will affect the grain pattern. A cut across the tree trunk will expose the circular annual rings and the rays show only as lines or narrow bands, or end grain (surface A). Sawing the log through the center or lengthwise, called "plain sawing," will show as highly figured lines or bands (surface B). If the same longitudinal cut is made away from the center, another pattern will result—now the rings will appear as broad stripes or patches while the rays will be narrow (surface C). A cut made on an angle to the heartwood, called "quartersawing" exhibits a linear pattern (surface D). Quartersawn wood is more expensive because there is more waste.

*Veneers.* Scarce and valuable woods with beautiful figuring and grain are frequently cut into veneers which are thin slices of the wood rather than board thickness. The thin veneer layers are then laminated, or applied, to the surface of cheaper timber by gluing and clamping. When you select a veneer, the stability of the veneer and the base wood are important so that neither shrinks away from the other. Veneers should be stored flat and in a dry place until they are to be used. It is also possible to create your own "veneers" of intricate laminates as shown in several examples by William Asquith Evans throughout the book. Often Mr. Evans's intricate laminates are sliced thin and placed over other woods to create the outer surfaces of his objects rather than using the laminated thickness for the entire object.

## MOISTURE CONTENT AND CURING

The water content of wood is of great importance. It affects the weight, size, shape, hardness, strength, and stiffness of the piece as well as its vulnerability to attacks by fungi and insects. The water content also determines the changes in these characteristics that will occur when the wood is transported to another environment. The manner in which the wood is dried affects its usability.

A tree's moisture content may range from about 30 percent to 200 percent of the weight of the wood substance. The wood is dimensionally stable when the moisture content is above the fiber saturation point. It changes dimension as it gains or loses moisture below that point. The drying and curing of wood to minimize quick shrinking and resulting checks is extremely important. Eliminating moisture is done by careful seasoning of the cut logs. Lumber companies are able to reduce the amount of shrinkage and cracking by various production methods. Logs may be immersed in water until they are ready for the sawmill, then sawn into boards. Drying may be accomplished by placing stacked boards outdoors in the air, by kiln drying, and by radio-frequency dielectric procedures. Industrial curing methods can be further investigated in books that deal with the technology and production of lumber.

The craftsman becomes involved in seasoning wood when he gathers his own logs. The small object maker is more fortunate than the person who makes huge sculptures or gathers wood for furniture; small objects can often be made from branches that dry more rapidly than entire logs. The seasoning time generally used for air drying is one year per inch radius. Working on green wood is a waste of time.

Logs that are left to cure should be placed off the ground so they won't

Appearances of different saw cuts.

Exploded view of the cambium layer.

The cambium layer is a single layer of living cells that extends from the tips of the tree's roots to the ends of the branches. During the tree's summer growth these cells continually divide and add only thickness but no height to the tree. The cells that form on the outside of the cambium layer become bark, those that form on the inside become wood.

*Courtesy, St. Regis Paper Co.*
*New York*

rot. In climates where winter weather and moisture are ever-present, wood is placed in curing sheds or barns to dry. Logs should usually be dried with the bark on; if the bark is removed, drying may occur too rapidly and result in severe radial checks that may begin in the sapwood and move into the heartwood. If insects exist in the bark it may be necessary to remove the bark. Insecticides may help but not always. Check manufacturers' labels for duration of insecticide life and use judiciously if objects made from the wood will be used for food. Freshly cut logs may be sealed to inhibit the rapid drying time that causes checks by brushing hot melted paraffin on the cut surfaces or covering the log ends with heavy plastic to hold in the moisture. Commercial wood sealers are also available. Only the cut ends and surfaces should be sealed, never the bark. Bark, nature's protective coating during growth, also protects the cut log from drying too rapidly.

## WHERE TO GET WOOD

Logs can be secured from a variety of sources such as farms, tree surgeons, city dumps, and lumber mills. Some tree limbs have a large enough circumference for the object maker, and these can be found after heavy storms. They must be allowed to cure, of course, before using. It is a good idea to learn to identify woods to be sure they are what you want before you go to the effort of cutting, hauling, and curing them. There are several books available that give keys and charts identifying timbers by their outstanding characteristics and these are offered in the bibliography. Generally the main keys are: primary color, secondary color, pattern of growth rings, pores, grain, hardness, weight, smell, bark, shape of leaf, country of origin, and class of use.

Cut board is available from lumberyards. More exotic species can be ordered by mail from suppliers listed in the Sources for Supplies. Your lumberman should be consulted for special buys in small quantities or for individual woods he can order specifically for your use.

The creator of small objects can use old wood from houses, hotels, and other public buildings that have been hit by the wrecker's blocks. Many wrecking companies keep stacks of scrap wood left over from stair posts, fireplaces, decorative woodwork. Often, the original use of the wood will be a clue to whether it is a softwood or hardwood and what kind. Painted scrap woods will be difficult to detect, but stripping the paint from an old chest of drawers, the backboard of a bar, or other old item may reveal a bounty of good mahogany, walnut, birch, and others. Finding the source for woods, the varieties of woods, and how to work them is often as challenging as the project itself.

## WORKING WITH WOOD

### Woodworking tools

Wood is man's oldest and one of his most useful natural resources. From the earliest times, man has fashioned wood for shelter, furniture, tools, and weapons. The story of early tools and how their shapes were developed from iron and wood has been covered in history and technology books and in museum exhibits of primitive man—all fascinating forays into the past. Considering that man has always used tools, we tend to forget that until quite recent times he depended entirely on hand tools to fell trees and work up their timber. It is hard to conceive that the abundance and scope of woodwork in the castles, churches, and other public buildings of the Romanesque,

# WOOD SELECTION CHART

| SPECIES | Comparative Weights[1] | Color[2] | Hand Tool Working | Nail Ability[3] | Relative Density | General Strength[4] | Resistance to Decay[5] | Wood Finishing[6] | Cost[7] |
|---|---|---|---|---|---|---|---|---|---|
| **HARDWOODS**[8] | | | | | | | | | |
| Apitong............ | Heavy | Reddish Brown | Hard | Poor | Medium | Good | High | Poor | Medium High |
| Ash, brown......... | Medium | Light Brown | Medium | Medium | Hard | Medium | Low | Medium | Medium |
| Ash, tough white.... | Heavy | Off-White | Hard | Poor | Hard | Good | Low | Medium | Medium |
| Ash, soft white...... | Medium | Off-White | Medium | Medium | Medium | Low | Low | Medium | Medium Low |
| Avodire........... | Medium | Golden Blond | Medium | Medium | Medium | Low | Low | Medium | High |
| Balsawood......... | Light | Cream White | Easy | Good | Soft | Low | Low | Poor | Medium |
| Basswood.......... | Light | Cream White | Easy | Good | Soft | Low | Low | Medium | Medium |
| Beech............. | Heavy | Light Brown | Hard | Poor | Hard | Good | Low | Easy | Medium |
| Birch............. | Heavy | Light Brown | Hard | Poor | Hard | Good | Low | Easy | High |
| Butternut......... | Light | Light Brown | Easy | Good | Soft | Low | Medium | Medium | Medium |
| Cherry, black...... | Medium | Medium Reddish Brown | Hard | Poor | Hard | Good | Medium | Easy | High |
| Chestnut.......... | Light | Light Brown | Medium | Medium | Medium | Medium | High | Poor | Medium |
| Cottonwood....... | Light | Greyish White | Medium | Good | Soft | Low | Low | Poor | Low |
| Elm, soft grey...... | Medium | Cream Tan | Hard | Good | Medium | Medium | Medium | Medium | Medium Low |
| Gum, red.......... | Medium | Reddish Brown | Medium | Medium | Medium | Medium | Medium | Medium | Medium High |
| Hickory, true...... | Heavy | Reddish Tan | Hard | Poor | Hard | Good | Low | Medium | Low |
| Holly............. | Medium | White to Grey | Medium | Medium | Hard | Medium | Low | Easy | Medium |
| Korina............ | Medium | Pale Golden | Medium | Good | Medium | Medium | Low | Medium | High |
| Magnolia.......... | Medium | Yellowish Brown | Medium | Medium | Medium | Medium | Low | Easy | Medium |
| Mahogany, Honduras | Medium | Golden Brown | Easy | Good | Medium | Medium | High | Medium | High |
| Mahogany, Philippine | Medium | Medium Red | Easy | Good | Medium | Medium | High | Medium | Medium High |
| Maple, hard........ | Heavy | Reddish Cream | Hard | Poor | Hard | Good | Low | Easy | Medium High |
| Maple, soft........ | Medium | Reddish Brown | Hard | Poor | Hard | Good | Low | Easy | Medium Low |
| Oak, red (average).... | Heavy | Flesh Brown | Hard | Medium | Hard | Good | Low | Medium | Medium |
| Oak, white (average).. | Heavy | Greyish Brown | Hard | Medium | Hard | Good | High | Medium | Medium High |
| Poplar, yellow....... | Medium | Light to Dark Yellow | Easy | Good | Soft | Low | Low | Easy | Medium |
| Prima Vera........ | Medium | Straw Tan | Medium | Medium | Medium | Medium | Medium | Medium | High |
| Sycamore.......... | Medium | Flesh Brown | Hard | Good | Medium | Medium | Low | Easy | Medium Low |
| Walnut, black...... | Heavy | Dark Brown | Medium | Medium | Hard | Good | High | Medium | High |
| Willow, black...... | Light | Medium Brown | Easy | Good | Soft | Low | Low | Medium | Medium Low |
| **SOFTWOODS**[9] | | | | | | | | | |
| Cedar, Tennessee Red | Medium | Red | Medium | Poor | Medium | Medium | High | Easy | Medium |
| Cypress............ | Medium | Yellow to Reddish Brown | Medium | Good | Soft | Medium | High | Poor | Medium High |
| Fir, Douglas........ | Medium | Orange-Brown | Medium | Poor | Soft | Medium | Medium | Poor | Medium |
| Fir, white.......... | Light | Nearly White | Medium | Poor | Soft | Low | Low | Poor | Low |
| Pine, yellow longleaf.. | Medium | Orange to Reddish Brown | Hard | Poor | Medium | Good | Medium | Medium | Medium |
| Pine, northern white.. (Pinus Strobus) | Light | Cream to Reddish Brown | Easy | Good | Soft | Low | Medium | Medium | Medium High |
| Pine, ponderosa...... | Light | Orange to Reddish Brown | Easy | Good | Soft | Low | Low | Medium | Medium |
| Pine, sugar......... | Light | Creamy Brown | Easy | Good | Soft | Low | Medium | Poor | Medium High |
| Redwood.......... | Light | Deep Reddish Brown | Easy | Good | Soft | Medium | High | Poor | Medium |
| Spruces (average).... | Light | Nearly White | Medium | Medium | Soft | Low | Low | Medium | Medium |

[1] Kiln dried weight.

[2] Heartwood. Sap is whitish.

[3] Comparative splitting tendencies.

[4] Combined bending and compressive strength.

[5] No wood will decay unless exposed to moisture. Resistance to decay estimate refers to only heartwood.

[6] Ease of finishing with clear or "natural" finishes.

[7] Prices for best grade.

[8] Leaf bearing tree.

[9] Cone and needle bearing trees.

WOOD SELECTION CHART, *Courtesy, Frank Paxton Lumber Company, Chicago*

Renaissance, and Gothic periods were all accomplished with simple tools. With our dependence upon power equipment, it is almost inconceivable that man could accomplish so much without machinery and electricity.

The Industrial Revolution encouraged the invention of woodworking machinery. The first woodworking machines are believed to have been developed in Holland as early as 1777, and a planing machine was patented in England about the same time. By the early part of the nineteenth century a wide range of versatile machines was designed to shape wood into useful products. The basic categories of woodworking machinery developed then are still essentially the same. Power, modern design, and myriad attachments have been added for further versatility. Most of the machinery can be seen in use in various demonstrations throughout the book. The woodworker can find them all pictured in catalogs and in the shop sections of department stores and machinery companies.

SAWING MACHINES:  The four commonest types are:
1) The *circular or table saw.* This machine cuts wood by means of a thin circular blade with teeth around its edge. The blade which protrudes through an opening in the table can be raised or lowered to make different depth cuts. Circular saws are classified according to the blade diameter, ranging from a small 8-inch bench saw to the 14-to-16-inch saws used in lumberyards and woodworking industries.
2) The *radial arm saw* does the same kind of cutting and uses the same type of blade as the circular saw but differs in design. The motor and blade are suspended under an arm above the table and mounted so they can be moved toward or away from the operator. The arm can be turned in a complete circle. The motor and blade can be turned through a complete horizontal circle and tilted in either direction giving the saw three-dimensional movement.
3) The *band saw* blade is a continuous metal band that runs around two large wheels. The blade has teeth along one edge. The band saw is capable of only a few operations but very important ones. It can cut curves in any thickness of stock. It can also be used for resawing boards to thinner dimensions. The blade makes a narrower kerf (the cut made by the saw) than the circular saw, so less wood is wasted.
4) The *jigsaw* does the same kind of cutting as the hand coping saw, making inside and outside irregular cuts. The blade is mounted between an overhead support and a driving mechanism that produces a reciprocating movement. The blade passes through an opening in a table upon which the work is manipulated.

PLANERS or SURFACERS are single-purpose machines for smoothing woods to an even thickness. There are a variety of models that range from a single planer which smooths one surface of a board at a time to machines that can finish all four surfaces simultaneously. The planer consists of a frame, a bed that can be moved up and down, and a cylindrical cutter head that holds three or more knives that pare off the excess wood.

JOINTERS are designed to smooth the surface, edge, or end of a board. The wood is pushed along a table over a rotating cutter head that flattens the wood so that it can be made to join perfectly with another piece of wood. They do the job done by a hand plane, but more efficiently.

A SHAPER consists of a table through which protrudes a rotating spindle carrying cutting blades. The blades are shaped to produce a specific contour on the work for making moldings, edge designs on furniture, picture frames, and so on.

An assortment of woodworking machines. *Front:* The circular, or table, saw. *Back, left to right:* A drill press, a shaper (behind are pipe and bar clamps), a belt sander, jigsaw, and jointer with a shop vacuum to pick up dust particles. Safety masks hang on the wall at right.

*Photographed at California State University, Long Beach*

A ROUTER is essentially an inverted shaper with the cutter spindle suspended over the work. It is used for carving lines and designs in surfaces.

LATHES. Long before any other woodworking machines were invented, the lathe was used to turn out cylindrical parts. A complete discussion of the lathe and its use will be found in chapter 3.

SANDERS are used to bring wood surfaces to a fine finish. There are several types: the belt sander which has a continuous strip of sandpaper running over two rollers; a disk sander which uses a piece of sandpaper fastened to a large metal disk, and the spindle sander, a cylindrical spindle around which a piece of sandpaper is fastened.

BORING MACHINES are used to bore the holes needed for dowel joints or for pegging (page 61).

The DRILL PRESS is an upright boring machine for making holes. A drill press can be provided with a variety of accessories to serve as a spindle sander, shaper, or router, and for making small and large circular cuts, and pegs.

MULTIPURPOSE machines are designed for home workshop or school use and perform many standard woodworking operations when used with a variety of attachments. Some models combine the functions of a drill press and lathe, as well as performing sawing and sanding procedures. Others are basically jigsaws, but attachments enable one to do sanding, routing, and a variety of other small carving procedures.

PORTABLE ELECTRIC tools are designed for convenience and ease of handling. They allow the machine to be brought to the work. The assortment of power hand tools offered by different manufacturers is large and varied. The five most common portable electric tools are: the handsaw for straight cutting; the saber or jigsaw for cutting irregular shapes; the router for making joints and shaping edges, grooves, and so on; the hand drill for boring holes; and sanders of pad, belt, and rotary types.

## Gluing

The use of fast-drying, transparent, permanent glues is an important factor for all types of woodworking. Many projects must have glued joints, glued members, veneers, and laminates. Some objects require gluing other materials such as plastics, metals, and papers to the wood surface. Finding the right glue to do the job is often a matter of experimentation with different types and brands. Sometimes one glue will work better on some woods than others.

Generally, the success of any glue operation is based on the following factors:
1) the adhesive selected
2) the type of wood and its proper preparation; joints must be clean and tight fitting
3) proper mixing or preparation of the glue
4) the application of the glue and the clamping operation
5) posttreatment and exposure condition of the glued member
6) the design of the joint or the laminate

The following glues are most often used by the craftsman working with small objects. Trade names vary and the same product may be packaged by different distributors. The information has been compiled by Lawrence B. Hunter.

LIQUID HIDE   Made from animal hides and bones
   Cost: Medium
   Temperature: 70° or above. Warm glue for cool temperature.
   Application: Apply thin coat to both surfaces. Let get tacky before joining.
   Assembly time: Short, about 5-10 minutes
   Clamping time: 2 hours minimum at 70°; Sears = 12 hours
   Characteristics: First choice for wherever a tough, lasting wood-to-wood bond is needed and for general wood gluing. Very strong because it is rawhide tough and does not become brittle. It is easy to use, light in color, resists heat and mold. It has good filling qualities, so gives strength even in poorly fitted joints. Not waterproof so do not use on objects to be placed outdoors.

## HAND TOOLS

Hand tools such as saws, drills, screwdrivers, chisels, miter boxes, and planes are readily available from local hardware dealers in a variety of sizes.

*Top left:* Hand tools have been used for wood carving for centuries by peoples of every culture. Different-shaped adzes are the primary tools still used by African woodcarvers to create an astonishing variety of objects.

*Collection, Frank E. Cumming III*
*Long Beach, California*

*Top right:* The sculptor's chisels and gouges assume an important role in the workshop of the object maker who combines carpentry with artistry.

*Bottom row:* Safety masks should be worn during sawing and other procedures that produce flying chips and dust. A full face mask is hinged so that in the down position it covers the entire face. It can be lifted when you are not working. Also available are goggles that fit only over the eyes and/or a pair of glasses that are held tightly to the head with an elastic band.

*Courtesy, Merit Abrasive Products, Inc.*
*California*

WHITE GLUE    White liquid resin or polyvinyl
              Made from chemicals
  Cost: Low
  Temperature: Any temperature above 60°, the warmer the better
  Preparation: Ready to use
  Application: Spread on both surfaces and clamp
  Assembly time: Very short, 5 minutes
  Clamping time: 2 hours at about 70°
  Characteristics: A fine all-around household glue for mending. Excellent
    for model work, paper, leather, and small assemblies. Not sufficiently
    moisture resistant for anything to be exposed to weather. Not so strong
    and lasting as Liquid Hide Glue for fine furniture work. Always ready to
    use at any temperature. Nonstaining, clean, and white. Quick-setting
    qualities recommend it for work where good clamping is not possible.
    High temperatures (100°+) tend to soften this adhesive. Very excellent
    for dowel-joint gluing since this adhesive does not become brittle.


CASEIN    Made from milk curd
  Cost: Low
  Temperature: Any temperature above freezing; however, the warmer the
               better
  Preparation: Stir together equal parts by volume of glue and water. Wait
               10 minutes and stir again.
  Application: Apply thin coat to both surfaces. Use within 8 hours after mix-
               ing.
  Assembly time: About 20 minutes
  Clamping time: 4-5 hours at 70°
  Characteristics: Will do most woodworking jobs and is especially desir-
    able with oily woods: teak, lemon, yew. Not moisture resistant enough for
    outdoor use. Will stain acid woods such as redwood. Must be mixed for
    each use. Works in cool locations, fills poor joints well. Casein glues will
    bond wood through a wide range of moisture contents from 2 to 20 per-
    cent. Two difficulties with casein glues are their abrasive effects on cut-
    ting tools and their wood-staining characteristics.


PLASTIC RESIN    Made from chemicals. "Weldwood," "Titebond"
  Cost: Medium
  Temperature: Must be 70° or warmer. Will set faster at 90°.
  Preparation: Mix 2 parts powder with 1/2 to 1 part water.
  Application: Apply thin coat to both surfaces. Use within 4 hours after mix-
               ing.
  Assembly time: About 20 minutes
  Clamping time: 16 hours at 70°
  Characteristics: Use it for woodworking and general gluing where con-
    siderable moisture resistance is wanted. Do not use with oily woods,
    such as teak, or with joints that are not closely fitted and tightly
    clamped. Must be mixed for each use. Very strong, although brittle if
    joint fits poorly. Light colored, almost waterproof. Mixing of the adhesive
    is somewhat difficult. Cleanup requires soap and warm water. Shelf life
    of the powder is good unless it becomes damp.

RESORCINOL    Made from chemicals. "Bordens," U.S. Plywood
  Cost: High
  Temperature: Must be 70° or warmer, will set faster at 90°
  Preparation: Mix 3 parts powder to 4 parts liquid catalyst.
  Application: Apply thin coat to both surfaces.
  Assembly time: 30 minutes to 1 hour
  Clamping time: 16 hours

CLAMPS
A variety of clamps may be employed for various gluing operations. Most wood shops are not so well equipped with the quantity and variety that Milon Hutchinson has, but knowing about clamps that may not be so readily available may help you solve stubborn and tricky gluing-clamping operations. Consult hardware catalogs for other types of clamps such as corner and mitering clamps.

Adjustable bar clamps and gluing clamps.

Metal-jaw bar clamps and spring clamps are on front table. C-clamps in assorted sizes hang at the back.

Industrially used lever-type clamps can be set up for convenient and quick application in the craftsman's workshop. Mr. Hutchinson has improvised and individualized boards with clamps screwed on for specific jobs.

The ultimate in the common hardwood jaw gluing clamp has been individualized by craftsman Walter C. Dreisbach who hand-carved the ends in the hand shapes.

*Courtesy, artist*

Characteristics: This is the glue for any work that may be exposed to soaking: outdoor furniture, boats, etc. Not good for work that must be done at temperatures below 70°. Because of dark color and mixing, not often used unless waterproof quality is needed. Very strong, as well as waterproof. It works better with poor joints than many glues do. Resorcinol creates a dark glue line.

EPOXY    Made from chemicals
Cost: Very high
Temperature:  Any temperature
Preparation:  Resin and hardener, mix in amounts stated on container.
Application:  Apply to both surfaces to be glued.
Assembly time:  Time varies, 1/2 to 1 hour
Clamping time:  Clamping is not necessary, sets faster with heat in about 24 hours.
Characteristics:  Will bond wood to metal or other dissimilar materials. Use in combination with wood, tile, metal, glass, etc. Will not shrink or swell during hardening. Waterproof, oilproof, and noninflammable. Not good for fastening wood in large products. Must be used in well-ventilated room. Avoid getting into eyes. Can be painted, sanded, filed, drilled, or machined. Can fill large holes. Excellent for poorly fitted joints. Do not use on flexible materials or where stress can peel it from the surface.

UREA-FORMALDEHYDE RESIN    Made from chemicals. Urac 185; Plyamine 21-018, Reichold Chemical Co.
Cost:  Medium
Storage Life:  6 months at 70° or below. Good as long as the liquid is pourable.
Preparation:  3 parts liquid to 1 part hardener

| Temperature: | 60 | 70 | 80 | 90 | 100 | Degrees |
|---|---|---|---|---|---|---|
| Assembly: | 40 | 30 | 20 | 10 | 5-10 | Minutes |
| Clamping: | 12 | 12 | 6 | 3 | 1½ | Hours |

Characteristics: Highly water resistant, flexible, craze resistant. Excellent for furniture, plastic laminates, and veneers. Good gluing characteristics where glue-line thickness and clamping pressure may vary. Glue-line thickness to .02″ is possible. Maximum strength is reached after 5 days at 70° or above.

Spread glue on broad surfaces easily with a roller. A broad spatula or brush will also do the job efficiently.

Edge gluing is easily accomplished with the tip of a glue bottle. A bar clamp holds the laminates until dry.

## Wood welding

Wood welding, called "dielectric heating" is based on the fact that disturbed molecules cause friction and create heat. The disturbed balance is caused by a very high frequency cycle change which moves the molecule of glue at such a high speed that the friction generates heat and the glue bond is completed in a matter of seconds.

The synthetic resorcinol and pheno-formaldehyde resins are easily cured with dielectric heating and are relatively immune to weather conditions. Urea-formaldehyde glues are less expensive than resorcinols but have similar qualities. Joints formed with urea resins are very resistant to heat and moisture. The strength of joints made with both types of glues increases with time.

Dielectric gluing is accomplished with a wood welding unit shown on page 67.

## Wood finishing

The cellular structure of wood requires the application of stains, fillers, varnishes, lacquers, paints, enamels, oils, or waxes to enhance the surface visually and totally and to protect the surface from dust and deterioration. Before applying finishes, carefully check all surfaces for dents, bumps, or stains. Sand off bumps. Raise dents by placing a damp cloth on the surface and touching it with the tip of a hot iron to expand the fibers.

Transparent and opaque wood finishes are applied by brushing, spraying, wiping, dipping, rolling, and rubbing. Finishes retard the absorption of moisture, fumes, and oils that cause the wood to shrink, swell, check, warp, and discolor.

Each woodworker seems to develop his own formula for finishing woods. The majority prefers natural oil finishes that bring out the natural grains and colors of fine woods. These vary from any proportion either side of 50-50 oil stain and raw or boiled linseed oil and turpentine to 100 percent linseed oil. Oil stains may be slightly pigmented or transparent. They are easily applied by brushing or wiping on. They preserve the wood and bring out the beauty without raising the grain and they produce a uniform tone or color.

Wood objects that will come in contact with food may be finished with vegetable cooking oils and reoiled frequently.

Varnish stains seal the wood and may produce various tonal changes without altering the grain. Aerosol foam and liquid stains offer great flexibility of application. Stains may also be made by thinning artists' oil paints with turpentine until they are fluid enough to be brushed or rubbed into the wood's surface and so penetrate the pores. Stained raw woods should be sealed with varnish, shellac, acrylic sprays, or epoxy finishes.

Coloring can be accomplished with any colorants available for wood such as enamels, paints, and acrylics. The wood must be sealed before applying the colorant. Carefully select the finish that will best serve your need; there are oil and water base, matte and gloss finishes, and the type you select will depend on the purpose of the finished item. Consider exposure to weather and humidity.

After applying the finish, a final rubbing with a fine pumice powder such as rottenstone mixed with linseed oil will reduce any fine paint bubbles or imperfections. Waxing with a good quality furniture wax is optional.

## Abrasive papers

Rough sanding and fine finishing are accomplished with abrasive papers used on sanding blocks, grinders, disk sanders, stationary and portable belt sanders. Abrasive grades during the finishing stages usually progress from coarse to fine. Final finishing may be done by hand rubbing with a fine powder such as rottenstone mixed with linseed oil. When choosing abrasives, there are three points to consider:

1) Open or closed coating. On a "closed coat," the abrasive grains are closely spaced, presenting a full surface. An "open coat" has spaces between the grains so that particles removed by sanding do not fill or clog the surface of the paper. This is desirable when doing round sanding or removing an old finish.

2) Correct abrasive. The minerals used in today's coated abrasives are an improvement over the crushed seashells once used. Those most often employed are: *aluminum oxide*, a manufactured abrasive good for wood and metal. It holds up well under power sanding and is used on hardwood, aluminum, copper, steel, ivory, and plastic. *Silicon carbide*, the hardest of all abrading materials, is good for sanding undercoats and for smoothing operations between coats. *Garnet* is generally used with power tools for abrading hardwood, softwood, composition board, plastic, and horn.

3) Correct grit. Various classifications of sandpaper can be broken down in terms of coarse, medium, and fine. Manufacturers have attempted to standardize the classification and symbols used on abrasive as shown in the accompanying chart.

## Abrasive papers

*Mesh numbers:* Abrasive grains are precision graded by passing them over a series of screens. Mesh numbers designate the grit sizes. For examples, grits that pass through a screen with 80 openings per linear inch are grit 80—designated as 80 (0). (0) is the symbol number.

| MESH NO. | SYMBOL | MESH NO. | SYMBOL |
|----------|--------|----------|--------|
| 600 | - | 100 | (2/0) |
| 500 | - | 80 | (0) |
| 411 | (10/0) | 60 | (1/2) |
| 360 | - | 50 | (1) |
| 320 | (9/0) | 40 | (1-1/2) |
| 280 | (8/0) | 36 | (2) |
| 240 | (7/0) | 30 | (2-1/2) |
| 220 | (6/0) | 24 | (3) |
| 180 | (5/0) | 20 | (3-1/2) |
| 150 | (3/0) | 16 | (4) |
| 120 | (0) | | |

*Courtesy, Norton Co., New York*

## MACHINING AND RELATED PROPERTIES OF HARDWOODS

| Kind of wood | Specific gravity based on green volume & oven dry wt. | Pounds/cu. ft. at 12% moisture control | Planing perfect pieces | Shaping good to excellent pieces | Turning fair to excellent pieces | Boring good to excellent pieces | Mortising fair to excellent pieces | Sanding good to excellent pieces | Steam bending unbroken pieces | Nail splitting pieces free from complete splits | Screw splitting pieces free from complete splits |
|---|---|---|---|---|---|---|---|---|---|---|---|
| | | | *Percent* | *Percent* | *Percent* | *Percent* | *Percent* | *Percent* | *Percent* | *Percent* | *Percent* |
| Alder, red | .37 | 28 | 61 | 20 | 88 | 64 | 52 | 75 | 67 | 65 | 71 |
| Ash | .54 | 41 | 75 | 55 | 79 | 94 | 58 | | | | |
| Aspen | .35 | 27 | 26 | 7 | 65 | 78 | 80 | 49 | 75 | 42 | 58 |
| Beech | .56 | 45 | 83 | 24 | 90 | 99 | 92 | 34 | 72 | 32 | 48 |
| Birch[1] | .60 | 46 | 63 | 57 | 80 | 97 | 97 | | | | |
| Cherry, black | .47 | 35 | 80 | 80 | 88 | 100 | 100 | 64 | 56 | 66 | 60 |
| Chestnut | .40 | 30 | 74 | 28 | 87 | 91 | 70 | | | | |
| Chinkapin | | | 75 | 25 | 77 | 90 | 90 | | | | |
| Cottonwood | .37 | 28 | 21 | 3 | 70 | 70 | 52 | 19 | 44 | 82 | 78 |
| Elm, soft | .46 | 36 | 33 | 13 | 65 | 94 | 75 | 66 | 74 | 86 | 74 |
| Gumbo-limbo | | | 80 | 20 | 60 | 60 | 80 | 50 | | | |
| Hackberry | .49 | 37 | 74 | 10 | 77 | 99 | 72 | | 94 | 63 | 63 |
| Hickory | .65 | 51 | 76 | 20 | 84 | 100 | 98 | 80 | 76 | 35 | 63 |
| Laurel, California | | | 40 | 60 | 86 | 100 | 100 | | | | |
| Madrone | | | 90 | 75 | 88 | 100 | 95 | | | | |
| Magnolia | .43 | 31 | 65 | 27 | 79 | 71 | 32 | 37 | 85 | 73 | 76 |
| Mahogany—African | .49 | 38 | 80 | 68 | 89 | 100 | 100 | | 41 | 68 | 78 |
| Maple, bigleaf | .44 | 33 | 52 | 56 | 80 | 100 | 80 | 38 | 57 | 27 | 52 |
| Maple, hard | .57 | 44 | 54 | 72 | 82 | 99 | 95 | 37 | 59 | 58 | 61 |
| Maple, soft | .56 | 44 | 41 | 25 | 76 | 80 | 34 | 81 | 86 | 66 | 78 |
| Oak, red | | | 91 | 28 | 84 | 99 | 95 | | | | |
| Oak, tanbark | | | 80 | 39 | 81 | 100 | 100 | | | | |
| Oak, white[2] | .59 | 47 | 87 | 35 | 85 | 95 | 99 | 83 | 91 | 69 | 74 |
| Pecan | .60 | 47 | 88 | 40 | 89 | 100 | 98 | | 78 | 47 | 69 |
| Sweetgum | | | 51 | 28 | 86 | 92 | 58 | 23 | 67 | 69 | 69 |
| Sycamore | .46 | 35 | 22 | 12 | 85 | 98 | 96 | 21 | 29 | 79 | 74 |
| Tupelo | | | 55 | 52 | 79 | 62 | 33 | 34 | 46 | 64 | 63 |
| Walnut, black | .34 | 26 | 62 | 34 | 91 | 100 | 98 | | 78 | 50 | 59 |
| Yellow-poplar | | | 70 | 13 | 87 | 87 | 63 | 19 | 58 | 77 | 67 |

[1] Includes yellow, sweet, and all other commercial birches except white or paper birch.
[2] Includes chestnut oak and other commercial white oaks.

Comparative physical properties of some popular woods. Data for this chart is from the U.S. Forest Products Laboratory and compiled by the Fine Hardwoods-American Walnut Association, Chicago, Ill. A more complete chart is available from the Fine Hardwoods-American Walnut Association booklet "Fine Hardwoods Selectorama."

# The Turned Wood Object

*Opposite:* By Jim Traynor. Lathe-turned and hand-finished wine decanter of East Indian rosewood. 8 1/2″ high, 3 1/2″ diameter. The goblets are exquisitely shaped, with British gray harewood cups and East Indian rosewood stems. (*See color photo for the complete table setting.*)

*Right:* A bud vase by Jim Traynor. Rosewood with shedua laminate and inlay, lathe turned. 12″ high, 3″ diameter.

*Below:* A simple, elegant, turned teak vase by Mel Mordaunt utilizes the grain pattern to emphasize the shaping. 4 3/4″ high, 4″ diameter.

The turned object refers to one that has been shaped on a lathe, perhaps one of the most versatile tools in the woodworker's shop. With the lathe, a block of wood can be quickly carried from rough form to finished work, including roughing, scraping, cutting, shaping, sanding, and oiling. The types of objects usually made on a lathe are spindles, bowls, cups, weed pots, bottles, beads, plates, and any items that fall within this shaping. The lathe also can be used to make asymmetrical turnings, ovals, and a variety of odd forms within the limitations of the tool's capabilities and the operator's capacity to experiment and improvise.

The lathe is a machine with two "centers" on a common horizontal axis between which material is held and rotated while being shaped with a variety of cutting tools. In addition to working material mounted between the two spindles, work can be mounted on faceplates which attach to the "live" or rotating center, so that flat projects such as bowls, plates, and hollow containers can be formed. Manufactured and improvised jigs may be attached in such a way that the work mounted on the lathe can be drilled and cut into in various ways, and its surface can have pegs, other wood inlays, and decorative embellishments.

The principle of the lathe has not appreciably changed since it was, reportedly, invented in ancient Egypt except that electric motors have replaced the hand or foot power used to turn the spindle. It still remains a means of turning work at controlled speeds, so that sharp tools pressed against it will cut it to a shape. The quality of the output depends on the forms the operator envisions and his skill in manipulating the chisels to release that vision from the rough block.

Wood lathes are designated according to the maximum diameter of work that can be swung over the bed; a lathe capable of swinging an 11-inch diameter disk of wood is called an 11-inch lathe. The terms *wood lathe* or *speed lathe* are usually used to avoid confusing them with screw-cutting, metal-turning lathes. The essential parts of the lathe are the *headstock*, the *tailstock*, and the *tool rest*. The two main attachments are the *spur center* that fits the headstock spindle and is known as the *live center* and the *cup center* that fits the tailstock spindle and is known as the *dead center.* The live center in the headstock serves as the driving unit that rotates the work while the dead center supports the opposite end. Attachments such as drill bits and boring units can be placed on the tailstock for making holes in ends and through the work.

Before operating a lathe, one should consult the manufacturer's directions and locate all the parts, learn how they work, and what they can do. For example, an indexing mechanism accurately spaced around the rim of the drive pulley can be used for spacing cuts in fluted work, for pegged inserts, and for dividing faceplate work.

One should understand the different rotating speeds. A good manual or handbook on the use of the lathe will inspire its application for asymmetric turnings and unconventional uses of the tools. Some are shown in relation to specific projects in this book, but it is wise to research many sources to spark additional ideas for your own work.

*Tools*: The standard set of tools used in wood turning includes five different shapes. Most important of these is the *gouge*, a roundnose, hollow chisel that can be used for any cutting action and especially for roughing cuts, cove cutting, turning work from square to round, and other operations. Next in importance is the *skew*, a double-ground flat chisel with the end ground to an angle instead of being square across. This tool is designed to cut, shear, and scrape and is used for smoothing cylinders, cutting shoulders, beads, V grooves, and so on. The *spear* or *diamond point* chisel and the *roundnose* are *scraping* tools used where their shape fits the contour of the work. The *parting tool* is a double-ground chisel used with a scraping action for cutting off and for making straight incisions or sizing cuts to any required diameter. All tools must be kept in optimum sharp condition.

The lathe is set on a table that can be either stationary or placed on wheels for mobility. Larry Hunter has utilized space beneath the table by building a holder for the tools where they are easily and safely accessible.

The parts of the lathe

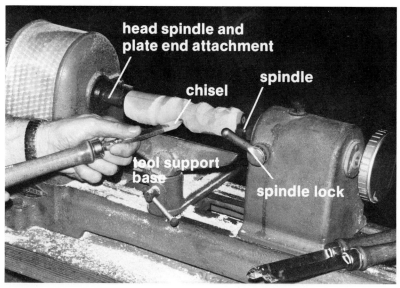

The *tool rest* consists of two main parts—the base and the tool rest, or support, itself. Different types of rests are interchangeable in the same base. One tool rest clamps onto the lathe bed and is used for turnings mounted between the spindles or on the headstock for chuck spindle turning. A floor stand for the tool rest is available for faceplate turnings. The tool rest should be about 1/8 inch away from and 1/8 inch above the work centerline.

The tool rest is designed to facilitate correct use of the hands and position of the tool. The back of the working hand, or a portion of it, rests on the finger ledge. The other fingers are placed comfortably around the tool. The other hand holds the handle of the tool and provides the movement that determines the cut. Generally the hand on the blade provides the action and the feed pressure, while the other hand acts as a control. Consider the area of the tool rest on which the chisel sits as a pivot point that is held by the thumb and fingers while the hand on the handle as actual control of the cutting edge.

The feed of the tool determines the amount of wood removed. It should be slow and steady, never forced or jabbed into the work.

There are three basic cutting actions—*scraping, cutting,* and *shearing.* Of the three, the *scraping* action is probably the easiest and most often used. The tool is held on a horizontal plane and moved directly forward into the work until the cut is the necessary depth. The full depth does not have to be reached at once. The chisel can be moved forward slightly, then moved from side to side, pivoting it on the point, achieving a shape at the same time the cut is being made.

For the *cutting* action, the tool edge is brought up by lowering the handle end of the chisel. The cutting action takes practice to master: if it is not done properly and the tool is jabbed into the wood too suddenly and deeply, it can be wrenched from your hands or you may lift a large splinter out of the work. But once the cutting action is mastered it can leave a surface smooth enough to be finished with little additional work.

A *shearing* action is usually accomplished with the skew and the gouge. It is like a cutting action with the tool moved parallel to the work as it shears away a layer of wood from the surface of the stock.

While each tool is intended for certain operations, their use can overlap and your choice of which tool to use for which job will depend on your facility, the cut to be made, and your eventual preference after you have practiced with them and their handling becomes second nature.

*Safety.* The lathe is a safe tool. The ultimate rule is never, never to work with dangling clothing such as neckties, necklaces, frayed or dangling sleeves, or with long, loose hair. Keep lathe chisels behind you or off to one side when you work so you won't have to reach over the turning work for a chisel when you need it. Never use your fingers to check the work for smoothness or roundness while the lathe is turning. Keep your chisels sharp for easy cutting, mount the work securely and run at the proper speed for the size of the work as indicated. Be sure the power switch is safely and easily accessible and attach a foot switch for ultimate convenience and safety.

The proper working position for lathe cutting is shown. The tool is held with one hand on the blade, the fingers resting on the tool rest. The other hand supports the handle which can be placed against the hip for stability. The handle is slightly lower than the cutting blade.

Basic and modified lathe cutting tools are:
A. Large, modified roundnose
B. Roundnose
C. Skew
D. Large gouge
E. Small gouge
F. Parting tool

G. Modified skewer
H. Roundnose from a file (ground on a grinder)
I.&J. Small roundnose forged from tool steel
K,L,M. Small lathe tools shaped on a grinder to various shapes for intricate work

*Opposite:* A few of the myriad types of items that can be turned on a lathe include spindles, furniture legs, tool handles, drawer and door pulls, mallets, dishes, and bowls.
*Courtesy, American Edelstaal, Inc.
Tenafly, New Jersey*

GRINDING AND SHARPENING
Lathe tools should be kept sharp for optimum cutting action. A grinding attachment
is available for the headstock of the lathe;
the tool rest can support and provide an adjustable base for mounting platforms made
especially to hold particular tools. Or use a
general purpose grinding wheel of a 60 grit
aluminum oxide about 5- to 6-inch diameter.
Always wear safety goggles when sharpening tools.

With the grinding wheel revolving toward
the operator, the tool is held low and gradually raised to a position in which the bevel
will lie flat on the stone. This angle is main-
tained throughout the grinding operation.
The roundnose, because it is convex on
the outside, must be rolled and worked from
one side of the stone to the other.

Continue to work the edge until the proper
cutting angle is achieved. A burr must remain
on the roundnose because it is essentially a
scraping tool.

A burr can be reset by passing the tool on
the concave side of a honing stone. When
any tool used for scraping is sharpened, the
burr should be left on. Cutting tools would
have the burr removed through honing.

## LATHE SPEED GUIDE FOR WOOD TURNING

Follow these recommended lathe speeds as nearly as possible. Change lathe speed only with the spindle in motion.

On pieces over 10″ diameter, keep the speed below the point where the lathe begins to vibrate.

## LATHE: WOOD TURNING
### Speed range of lathe: 230 RPM to 2100 RPM

| DIAMETER OF WORK | OFF ROUGHING | CUTTING GENERAL | FINISHING |
|---|---|---|---|
| Under 2″ | 900 RPM | 2100 RPM | 2100 RPM |
| 2″ to 4″ | 700 | 2100 | 2100 |
| 4″ to 6″ | 700 | 1200 | 2100 |
| 6″ to 8″ | 500 | 800 | 1250 |
| 8″ to 10″ | 350 | 700 | 900 |
| over 10″ | 230 | 350 | 600 |

Detail showing the proper edges of standard lathe-turning tools. Angles should be retained accurately when sharpening.

SKEW

ROUNDNOSE

SPEAR POINT

GOUGE

SQUARE NOSE

PARTING TOOL

There are many manufacturers of lathes. One usually thinks of a large unit that requires an ample workroom setup. A miniature unit that is used by several of the craftsmen whose work appears in this book is one which can be set up on a small worktable when space is limited. The Unimat, an amazingly versatile machine, has all the features of a large precision unit on a small scale. A variety of attachments can alter its performance as a lathe to a polisher grinder, drill press, vertical mill, or surface grinder. Available accessories include a planer, jointer, and other woodshop needs.

*UNIMAT set up as lathe*
*Courtesy of American Edelstaal, Inc.*
*Tenafly, New Jersey*

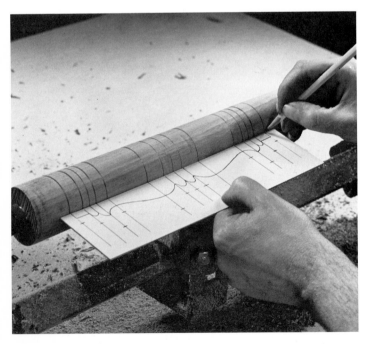

For spindle turning, a paper layout can be used for making several shapes the same.

The wood is placed between the tailstock and headstock and turning begins using a scraping tool to shape and smooth.

Sanding can be accomplished while the object is on the lathe.

A grinding wheel accessory attached to the headstock can be used to sharpen tools.
*UNIMAT setups in use*
*Courtesy of American Edelstaal, Inc.*
*Tenafly, New Jersey*

# TURNING A BOWL ON THE FACEPLATE

Turnings such as spindles, beads (see page 86), table legs, and posts are mounted between the two centers of the lathe. The shape may be formed in any limited area or along the entire length of the stock. Not all lathework is mounted between centers. Such items as bowls, plates, lamp bases, and so on must be mounted on a faceplate, attached only to the live center in the headstock.

Bowls are among the challenging and popular forms that craftsmen tackle. Large bowls are turned on the outboard end of the headstock. The method is demonstrated by Lawrence B. Hunter. Several examples of bowls created by many craftsmen follow the demonstration. After the bowl is turned, further designing, shaping, and surface decoration may be accomplished by direct carving with hand or power tools.

All cutting in faceplate work is done by scraping; any attempt to use a cutting technique on the edge grain of large work will result in a gouging cut that may pull the chisel out of your hands. The tool rest is placed on a floor stand.

The stock used may be from a log that has been roughly cut to shape on a band saw, from a block of solid wood, or from a block of laminated wood pieces.

Once the faceplate is mounted you should establish dimension lines for the depth of the cut and the thickness of the walls of the bowl. Dividers and compasses are helpful in measuring the work as it progresses and templates may be used as in spindle turning.

For reaching into deep, hollow projects, the straight tool rest is not always adequate support. Larry Hunter has fashioned a curved tool rest (page 55). In the series on page 61, photo shows how Milon Hutchinson has created a jig with a small blade for cutting deep, hollow interiors. It is possible that every woodworker who turns bowls has solved the problem in his own ingenious ways. These or any solutions may be adapted to your own working methods.

The following series is: a) mounting the faceplate to the end that will be the top of the bowl and finishing the base completely. b) Changing the faceplate to the finished base and then working the interior. The bottom is worked first because once the interior is hollowed out from the top of the bowl, there is no surface to which the faceplate may be attached for finishing the base.

The 6-inch faceplate is centered and screwed to a block of English walnut 7″ high and approximately 12″ in diameter. It is placed on the lathe and hand turned so that a pencil line circumference can be determined for the exterior diameter.

Above: The block is placed on the band saw and the excess diameter is cut away. The diameter is now 10''.

Right top: The block attached to the faceplate is placed on the outboard end of the headstock and scraping of the base begins. (See photo page 54 for overall working position.)

Right center: The base of the bowl begins to evolve. The roundnose is used exclusively with a scraping action.

Right below: The bottom is finished as much as possible. Sanding is accomplished with sanding disks mounted on a 1/4-inch drill. A flexible sanding disk is invaluable for achieving the subtle curves desired. Mr. Hunter attached a circle of 1/8-inch Masonite to a 1/4-inch bolt which is placed in the chuck. A slab of foam rubber is glued to the Masonite. Then a circle of inner tubing is glued to the foam. Use a strong glue for Masonite, foam, and inner tubing. A sanding disk is lightly glued to the inner tube so it can be changed easily. The sanding drum can be moved in any direction. One can make these in a range of diameters from 2'' to 6''. Hard disks already mounted to a bolt can be purchased and then fitted with the foam and tubing.

BOLT

MASONITE

FOAM

INNER TUBE

SANDING DISK

A

B

C

*Above:* a) The bottom is completed. The 6-inch faceplate is placed against the bottom and marked for central placement and holes. b) The holes are made with a drill. c) The faceplate is screwed on securely. When the bowl is completed the holes will be filled in with particles of sanded wood mixed with Duco cement (see page 78).

Mr. Hunter shows the working position and tool setup for outboard faceplate turning. He is beginning to scrape down the exterior shape. As the work proceeds, it's a good idea to take it off the lathe occasionally and set it upright to determine how the shape is evolving.

He begins to cut into the center to release the rim. When the tool dulls it must be sharpened on a grinder.

The rim is established so that hollowing out may be done. Cutting into this much wood is a slow procedure that should not be rushed.

He proceeds to hollow out the center. Instead of the straight tool rest, which does not give adequate tool support for deep interiors, Mr. Hunter uses a rounded rest which he made from a piece of scrap steel found in a junkyard to which he welded a piece of curved steel rod. Final sanding and oiling may also be done on the lathe (see pages 51, 77, and 88).

*Demonstration, Lawrence B. Hunter*
*Photos, author*

*Above:* By Dan L. Valenza. Turned bowl of walnut,
El Salvador Group. 8'' high, 11 1/2'' diameter.
*Collection, Smithsonian Institution*
*Photo, artist*

*Left:* By Lawrence B. Hunter. Shedua. Lathe-turned
bowl with hand-tooled gouge texture on outside.
3'' high, 14'' diameter.

*Right:* By Bob Stocksdale. Zebrawood with concen-
tric circles. 4'' high, 7 1/4'' wide, 6 1/2''
deep.

*Above:* Laminated walnut bowl by Charles M. Kaplan, 5″ high, 15″ diameter.

*Photo, artist*

*Below:* By Mark Lindquist. Turned spalted yellow birch bowl. 5 1/4″ high, 10″ diameter.

*Photo: Bob LaPree*

*Above:* By Lawrence B. Hunter. Bowl of worm-eaten California pepper. 4 1/2″ high, 7″ diameter.

*Below:* By Melvin and Mark Lindquist. Turned wild cherry burl bowl. 6″ high, 8″ diameter.

*Photo, Bob LaPree*

*Above:* Box by Milon Hutchinson. A round interior with a cover within a square base. Vermilion and padouk. 3 1/2'' high, 7 1/4'' square.

*Below:* By Lawrence B. Hunter. Teak. 7'' high. Graduated bowls up to 14'' diameter. The lathe-turned pedestals are carefully designed to form tiers.

*Left above:* By Irving Fischman. Bowl of laminated walnut, zebrawood, and teak. 9'' high, 9 1/2'' diameter. The shape is based on native American basketry concepts.                    *Courtesy, artist*

*Left center:* By Keith E. Stephens. Turned teak-wood bowl with hand-carved exterior. 4'' high, 12'' diameter.

*Left below:* Miniature corked jars and vase by Jay O'Rourke. Various woods: cocobolo, rosewood, Burmese padouk, osage orange, shedua. Vase is 2'' high, 3/4-inch diameter. Jars range from 1 1/4'' high, 1-inch diameter to 2'' high, 1 5/8'' diameter.

Three bowls of entirely different shapes made on a lathe. By Lawrence B. Hunter. English walnut. Sizes are 4″ high; 7″, 8″, and 10″ diameter.

*Below:* Mr. Hunter shows the method used for achieving the exterior texture with a narrow-blade gouge.

## TURNING A JAR SHAPE

Deep narrow boring is required for jars, boxes, and similar containers, and these may be done on the outboard of the faceplate as shown in the previous demonstration or on the inner turning spindle as illustrated here.

An item is placed on the turning spindle by any chucking method that will hold the cylinder firmly so it can be bored on the inside. The wood can be screwed directly to the faceplate. Another method is to glue a piece of paper between a piece of scrap wood and the turning wood. The latter procedure results in a perfectly finished bottom without the need for screw holes to be camouflaged and filled in later.

The following shows the methods for making deep borings with the object mounted on the inner turning spindle. You can proceed by cutting away the interior with lathe tools or by boring a hole in the center with a drill press and then using the lathe tool to work outward. Or you can devise your own tools such as that demonstrated at far right by Milon Hutchinson.

The wood piece is cut from the log on the band saw.

A piece of wood may be mounted so there are no faceplate screwholes in the finished base. The faceplate is mounted and screwed to a piece of scrap wood. A circle of paper is glued between the scrap wood and the wood to be turned, then clamped and allowed to dry thoroughly. After turning, the woods are separated at the paper line (see page 76, punch cup base demonstration).

Boring into the central opening is accomplished with the wood turning on the headstock spindle. The tool rest is clamped in the lathe base and moved to the necessary height and angle. The exterior of the shape is also cut while mounted in this fashion. All cutting is done by scraping with the roundnose, skew, or spear tools.

Because boring is a slow process that requires hand-holding the tool for long periods, Milon Hutchinson created a boring bar with a tool-steel cutting blade (*see below*) that simulates the cutting action of the lathe tool. It enables you to achieve a greater depth and a cleaner cut interior than a hand-held tool. The boring bar is made from a piece of curved pipe that is directed into the hollow by hand. The cutting action occurs along the interior side of the object as the blade is moved in and out. An adjustable stop ring (*just next to hand in photo*) adjusts the depth of the cut.

The crank, *lower left*, turns in a clockwise movement and adjusts the horizontal position of the boring bar. First a hole is drilled into the center of the object with a drill, then the hole can be quickly and easily enlarged with the boring tool.

The apparatus is made so that it is locked into the lathe bed with a wing nut, *bottom right*. Another lock fits through from the top for securing it to the lathe.

*Below:* In the circle you can see the blade which is a piece of cutting steel from a metal lathe that will cut metal as well as wood.

*Above:* Covered jar by Milon Hutchinson. Rosewood with teak band and handle. 9″ high, 3 3/4″ diameter. Interior carved to hold a glass condiment jar. Faceplate screwed on base is covered with an octagonal outer shape base.

*Top right:* By Lawrence B. Hunter. A covered container with a rosewood bottom and lignum vitae top. Leather lining. 5″ high, 4 1/2″ diameter.

*Below right:* By Lawrence B. Hunter. Turned bowl of avocado wood with chip-carved exterior. 4″ high, 5″ diameter.

*Above:* By Keith E. Stephens. Myrtlewood bowl and box. Each 5″ high, 5″ diameter.

*Below left:* By Charles M. Kaplan. Laminated cherry and walnut bowl. Lathe-turned interior, hand-carved exterior. 7″ high, 9″ diameter.

*Below right:* By Jocko Johnson. Ironwood cup. Interior machine turned with hand-carved base. 6″ high, 4″ diameter.

## DECORATIVE PEGGINGS

Many of the objects shown throughout the book have decorative surface treatments made by pegging, inlay, painting, nailing, carving, and so forth. In this demonstration, Milon Hutchinson shows the application of a variety of inlaid plugs, some in single and some in double rows; some double cut one within another. Mr. Hutchinson applies this plugging to jars and bowls. In several, the plugging appears only on the outside, in others, they go all the way through. In other motifs, only some of the plugs appear on the interior and exterior. The range of possible combinations is unlimited.

Such plugging must be measured accurately and spaced, or indexed, around the object. The main procedures that must be accomplished are a) indexing, b) boring the holes, and c) making and placing the pegs.

Indexing can be accomplished in several ways, and Mr. Hutchinson demonstrates indexing with a circular indexing device that he has devised and with the lathe. He demonstrates boring holes on the boring machine and on the lathe. Indexing and boring can also be accomplished on a drill press but not as accurately or easily as on the other two tools. Pegs can be made from ready-made dowels or created with the plug cutter as shown in photos on page 66. Then they are hand-set. Plugs are placed in the partially turned object. After the plugs are set, final turning is done to smooth the plugs on the outside, and on the inside where necessary.

Pegged inlay jars hold glass liners for jelly or other foods. By Milon Hutchinson. *Left jar:* Monkeypod with teak peg inlays and Brazilian rosewood lids. *Right jar:* Monkeypod with a purpleheart lid. The outer circular inlay is rosewood with a white maple inner plug. 6'' high, 2 3/4'' diameter.

An indexing ring with holes bored around the circumference is clamped to the adjustable table of the boring unit. The object is secured to the indexer by a tight-fitting inner chuck. The boring machine is set at a 1/2-inch depth cut and the drill is 5/8 inch.

An index locking lever is used, *at right*, to secure the unit while the hole is being bored. The adjustable table permits the unit to be raised and lowered to make holes at different levels in the object without replacing and realigning the indexer.

Mr. Hutchinson checks the progress of the drill along the marked lines. It is easier and more efficient to drill with an object flat on a table than holding it up in a drill press.

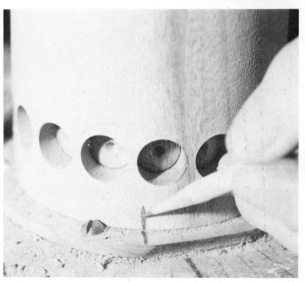

When the boring of the first row of holes is completed, mark the object in relation to the table so that you can replace it in the same position if you wish to do a second row of holes, or of smaller holes within the first pegs.

The bored holes are ready to receive the pegs. Pegs are quickly made using a 5/8-inch plug cutter along a 3/4-inch strip of wood.

When a series of plugs are cut, the strip is run through the blade on the table saw. Store extra pegs of each type of wood in jars labeled with name of wood and diameter of peg.

An industrial glue, San-o-Lac, is distributed around the edge of the hole with a dowel of a smaller diameter than the hole.

The pegs are driven into the hole with a hammer. Plugs are usually contrasting colors and grain for distinctive variations.

If plugs are too tight sometimes an air compression occurs and the plug blows back out. The peg can be seated using a C-clamp for a few seconds until the compressed air dissipates.

After all plugs are seated and thoroughly dried, the jar is placed on the lathe for final turning and smoothing around the pegged area and anywhere else additional shaping is desired.

Gluing can also be done with an electronic glue welder which heats and dries the glue instantly. (Hand gluing requires that you wait for the glue to dry before finishing on the lathe.) The electronic wood welder works with heat induction and requires a special glue. On this jar, one series of pegs has been finished flush with the jar, and a second series of pegs has been inlaid partially within the first series.

*Demonstration: Milon Hutchinson*
*Photos, author*

All items on these pages are by Milon Hutchinson and illustrate various applications of decorative pegging.

*Above:* Bowl of African laurel with a single row of rosewood pegs. 1 5/8" high, 7 1/2" diameter.

*Left:* Covered jar of monkeypod with teak and Brazilian rosewood pegs and rosewood lid. A single row of pegs is at top of body, a double row of superimposed pegs at bottom. First a row of 1/2-inch pegs were worked in, then overdrilled with a row of 5/8-inch pegs. A matching double peg is in top center of lid.

*Opposite top:* A rosewood bowl with teak inlay. 1 5/8" high, 9" diameter. The first row of pegs was placed through the bowl rim to show on inside and out. The second row was inlaid only in the outer surface of the bowl.

*Opposite below:* Teak bowl with rosewood inlay. 5 1/2" high, 7 1/2" diameter. Elongated pegs were cut on a drill press. Indexing and boring also accomplished on the drill press.

In this series Milon Hutchinson shows how a bowl is mounted, indexed, and bored using the lathe.

The bowl blank is held to a piece of scrap wood using glued paper sandwiched between. The scrap wood is mounted to the faceplate.

Indexing is accomplished using the indexing dial on the lathe.

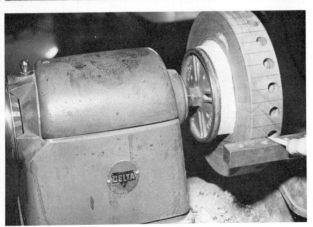

The bowl block is mounted on the lathe and, as the indexing unit is spaced (*left*), a line is drawn on the bowl using the tool rest as the ruler. Here one set of holes has been bored and lines are indexed for the second set which will be placed between and slightly below those in the first row.

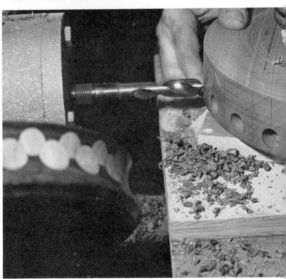

With a boring unit the holes are drilled around the circumference of the bowl with the bowl placed in a horizontal position. The result will be the double inlay peg shown in the bowl edge held at left in the photos and in the finished bowl (*top of page 69*).

When a boring machine is not available, holes can be made using an improvised setup on the lathe. First, holes are bored in a small block of hardwood such as maple, using a drill press with the desired diameter bit. The piece then serves as a jig, and it is clamped to the tool rest so the hole lines up with the position of the bowl set up on the inner center of the lathe.

The bowl is positioned and tightened, and the hand drill is worked through the hole in the jig into the bowl. Put a stop washer on the drill bit so it stops at the depth desired.

Mr. Hutchinson has also developed a method for drilling square holes. He made a special fixture for use on the boring machine. Using a square mortising tool from the drill press, he outfitted the end fixtures so they could be placed on the boring machine. A drill bit is placed within the mortising tool. When the bit is worked into the wood, the mortising square punches through resulting in a square hole that is then inlaid with square dowels. The bowl, *right*, still on the lathe shows the combination of round and square pegs inlaid.

*Demonstration: Milon Hutchinson*
*Photos, author*

By Mel Mordaunt. Maple vases with various inlays. *Left:* a pau ferro line and maple center. 3″ high. *Center*, Padouk inlays. 5″ high. *Right*, Brazilian rosewood inlays. 3″ high. All 3 1/4″ diameter.

*Courtesy, artist*

Mel Mordaunt has developed methods for insetting various geometric shapes of different woods in his beautifully designed weed pots. He says, "I like my work to be simple, clean, and crisp rather than ornate or complicated. Within this structure I wanted some sort of surface decoration. This solution was inspired by some of the Swedish glass designs with a symmetrical motif repeated around the circumference."

To accomplish insets, Mr. Mordaunt uses a router guided by an improvised jig that fastens and locks onto his lathe. He demonstrates the entire procedure in the following pictures.

First the overall shape is roughed out of a block of East Indian rosewood shown set up for spindle turning on the lathe. By shaping first, he knows approximately how deep and long to make the grooves for the insets.

To cut the grooves, Mr. Mordaunt has fashioned a jig of 5/8-inch plywood to guide the router. *At left:* the cover has been removed from the headstock to show the index pulley inside, which has been premarked to various divisions of 360° (8, 12, 16, 24) evenly spaced around it. The artist had to create a "spacer" (a fat plywood washer) between the lathe shaft and faceplate so the cut would go far enough toward the vase's bottom.

The router is held with the base against the jig and the bit extending through the jig. Strips on each edge of the jig serve as the guide for pulling the router evenly along the cut to be made. The indexing pulley has been locked into position to prevent the vase from rotating. The jig is adjustable to various angles for a variety of shaped cuts, shown in the vases at left, opposite.

*Above:* The 1/2-inch-diameter router bit has created several cuts. The 90° end of the bit cuts the wood at an angle so that a V groove is produced rather than a rectangular slot.

*Right:* After a groove is cut, the jig continues to hold the bit perfectly perpendicular to the vase; the vase is rotated on the preset mark, and the next groove is cut.

Small maple insets are sanded to the precise angle of the groove made in the vase, using a sanding disk and table on the lathe. Mr. Mordaunt uses an icepick rather than his fingers to hold the maple insets against the sander.

Glue is spread around the edges of the grooved recesses, and the insets are pressed tightly into place. The widths of the insets must be carefully measured so they lie next to one another (and do not overlap) when placed around the vase.

All insets have been glued into place. After they are completely dry, the unit is ready for turning.

Turning is accomplished using the conventional turning methods until the insets are flush with the vase. Insets must be thoroughly glued and dried or they will chip out during turning.

After they are turned, the insets begin to have the appearance of their final form. However, further turning will be done to finish shaping the vase.

The finished vase of rosewood and maple, by Mel Mordaunt, shows the change it has undergone in shaping from the original block and how the placement of the insets has beautifully enhanced the surface.

*Demonstration: Mel Mordaunt*
*Photos, author*

## LAWRENCE HUNTER TURNS AND
## SPINS A SET OF PUNCH CUPS

Punch cup set by Lawrence B. Hunter. The lathe has been used for turning the variety of different wood bases in a conventional wood turning technique. The cups are also made on the lathe by a metal spinning process illustrated in the pages that follow.

The base is made from a block cut out to the same diameter as the faceplate. The faceplate is used for a guide. It may be attached to the block before cutting out so it is perfectly centered on the block or it may be attached after the block has been cut.

The 3-inch faceplate and 2-inch backing block are attached to a piece of wood of smaller diameter, with a piece of paper glued between the two. This permits a clean parting of the two pieces of wood and eliminates the hole marks that remain when the faceplate is glued to the block.

With the block attached to the lathe, a 1/4-inch drill is placed in the chuck and put on the tailstock. A small hole is drilled in the end of the block so the block can be stabilized in the lathe while turning takes place.

With the block stabilized, shaping proceeds with the conventional lathe cutting tools.

When shaping is completed, sanding with various grades of papers can be easily and evenly done while the object is spinning on the lathe.

Rubbing in finishing oils is also efficiently accomplished on the lathe. Place the oil on a cloth and hold against wood. Buff with a Kleenex tissue.

To separate the finished form from the plate, place a wood chisel on the paper separator line. Tap the top of the chisel with a mallet until the base separates from the block.

The paper will split. The paper and glue can be sanded off, and the bottom finished for a perfectly crafted base.

If you decide to screw the faceplate to the block as opposed to gluing a piece of parting paper between the two, sanded particles of the wood should be collected and placed in a jar.

When the block is removed, the particles of wood can be mixed with Duco cement, or other glue, to the consistency of a wood paste filler and placed in the holes, then sanded and finished.

## METAL SPINNING THE CUP ON THE LATHE

Spinning metal on the lathe is a challenging use of the tool. It permits the artist to combine metals with a variety of woods, and many objects can be created. "Spinning" differs from the usual concept of lathework in that the metal is formed over a shape (called a chuck) rather than being cut away. Accessory equipment required for spinning is a ball bearing live center as well as a special type of tool rest with a fulcrum pin (seen in photos on page 81) that allows the tool to be moved evenly across the work. The tools are basically a *flat tool* and a *point tool*. The flat tool is actually round on one side and flat on the other. The round side is used to break down the metal blank against the chuck surface and the flat side is used for smoothing. The *point tool* is both a forming and finishing tool. A *beading tool* is also used to turn the rim of a metal disk into a lip or true bead. All spinning tools must be hardened steel and highly polished to avoid friction or marking the work. They may be purchased or made from 3/8-inch rod steel by heat forging, shaping, and polishing.

A back stick made of wood is also used to support the metal disk from the back during the spinning operation. It is simply a length of wood that can be made from an old broom handle and sharpened to a dull flat pointlike chisel. Its use is demonstrated in the photo series.

Any soft sheet metal can be spun. Brass is used for the punch cups shown, but one can also spin pewter, aluminum, and copper. Silver or gold may be used, but their cost makes them prohibitive. The gouges commonly used run from 16 to 22. Brass and copper require more frequent annealing than pewter or aluminum.

The materials required for making the brass punch cups include a chuck the shape of the finished cup, the flat tool, and the beading tool. The metal pieces show the progression of the shaping from flat disk to the finished cup.

The chuck, shaped of hardwood on the lathe, should be about an inch or so longer than the proposed spinning so there will be some space between the finished spinning and the faceplate. A metal lathed piece the same shape is also required for planishing shown on page 84, bottom left. It is cut on a metal lathe.

## PREPARING THE BLANK

A 5-inch diameter circle is inscribed on the brass sheet with a compass. In all spinning, the radius of the blank should be equal to the radius of the project plus the depth of the project. The blank should form a perfect circle with a smooth edge all around.

A dot is made from the compass center of the paper template through to the brass to position the center later. Paper templates help determine how to get the most circles out of a sheet before cutting.

With an aviation snip, the brass is cut around the outer edge of the inscribed line. The line should remain as a guide for filing to an even, smooth edge after spinning is completed.

A dimple is dapped into the disk at the center with a 1/4-inch punch. This fits into a concave mark on the chuck and prevents the disk from slipping.

The flat disks are annealed by heating with the soft flame of an oxyacetylene torch, with a propane torch or other heat supply. Annealing softens the metal and keeps it in a working condition. It is heated to a dull red, air cooled slightly, then dipped into a pickling solution.

Pickling involves dipping the metal in a solution of 5 percent sulphuric acid/95 percent water, or a commercial pickling solution, and then rinsing in running water. Annealing must be done frequently during the spinning process because the change in molecular structure causes the metal to harden, become brittle and crack. With practice, you can detect stiffness and resistance of the metal during spinning and that calls for annealing.

The disk is placed on the chuck on the lathe (*see next photo also*) for positioning. Observe the tool rest with the movable fulcrum pin. The ball bearing center should be brought up snugly against the disk and rotated to be sure it is properly centered. If not, the disk will get an off-center shape.

After positioning, and each time after annealing and before spinning, the outside surface should be lightly coated with grease applied with a cloth. Mr. Hunter uses a 90 weight automotive grease and just enough to allow the tool to slide over the surface without abrasion.

## SPINNING INTO SHAPE

The first operation employs the flat tool placed on the tool rest between the fulcrum pin and the disk. During the spinning, observe how the fulcrum pin is moved out along with the working position to yield good leverage for the tool. Use one or two sweeping strokes off the round side of the flat tool to seat the disk against the chuck. Hold the back stick against the metal on the chuck side while the spinning disk is pressed against the opposite side. The lathe speed is about 700 RPM.

Each time the spinning begins, the tool is placed at the very center and worked down against the chuck in a back and forth movement over each area. The outer part of the metal must be kept straight like a shallow funnel and not allowed to bell out. If belling begins to occur, immediately spin the rim to a straight funnel shape.

Spinning employs two essential operations that are repeated until the required shape is achieved: crowding a small portion of the metal to the chuck surface and keeping the rest of the disk funnel shaped. The shape must be formed slowly and gradually. If you bear down and form the shape in a couple of minutes, the metal will thin and buckle.

When the metal begins to resist the shaping, it must be removed from the chuck and annealed and pickled. Here you can see the disk partially shaped in a gradual funnellike angle. When replaced on the lathe, it must be regreased.

At this point half of the cup is against the chuck. The chuck acts as the backing for the lower part, but as the tool is moved against the metal where it has not been worked to the chuck, the backing stick must be ready to place between the metal and the chuck.

The metal is spun totally against the chuck and shaping is completed. The skew is used to cut off excess metal and yield an even rim. Leather gloves should be worn during this cutting operation as a piece of metal could fly off and lodge in the hand.

FILING AND PLANISHING

The rim edge is sharp, rough, and flat when removed from the chuck. The edge should be filed from the outside to the inside until it is dull when you run your finger along it.

The file end is covered with a piece of tape so that when you file toward the inner part of the bowl you won't mar the metal should the file slip.

Planishing consists of flattening small metal areas with a hammer to remove the spinning marks and yield an interesting texture. One can leave the spinning marks if desired, or combine spinning marks and planishing.

Planishing is done over a dome-shaped support (which has been turned on a metal lathe to approximate the shape of the cup) set on the end of a metal stake secured in a vise.

## SOLDERING THE STEM

Mr. Hunter has devised a soldering stand for easy positioning and soldering a length of 1/4-inch brass rod to the bottom of the cup. The horizontal wood shape slides up and down on the dowel at right. A screw eye at the left enables him to hold and lightly adjust the rod onto the cup which is placed on a piece of asbestos on the base piece of wood.

The brass rod is sawed to the proper length with a jeweler's saw. It is held securely by another invented apparatus made from a piece of wood clamped in the vise. The wood has a split and 1/4-inch keyhole-shaped jaw to accept the brass stem.

A slot is made in the stem of the punch cup. The wood base has a 1/4-inch hole. By spreading the brass stem slightly it will be compressed tightly in the hole and prevent the wood base from falling off the punch cup when it is in use.

The finished spun metal cup, now cleaned and polished, is placed in the turned wood base and the cup is complete.

*Demonstration: Lawrence B. Hunter*
*Photo series, author*

## SPINDLE TURNING

The demonstrations so far have shown how to shape and bore bowls, jars, and cup bases. The basic cutting methods can be applied to achieve a variety of interesting forms for useful objects. Lawrence Hunter uses the techniques normally associated with spindle cutting but achieves a sculptural form that can be cut off at any point and perhaps drilled for a candlestick holder or a dried weed pot. When the shapes are completely severed from one another, beads can be made. With imagination, the approach can be applied to scores of objects or for embellishments such as decorative knobs, pulls, feet for other useful objects, and for jewelry.

With practice, the shapes can be made by eyeballing the turning for evenness, or one can cut a piece of heavy paper and make a template to hold against the wood and test the shaping during the turning.

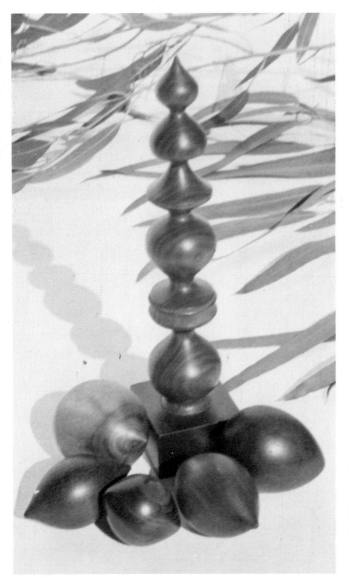

Sculptural decorative forms. By Lawrence B. Hunter. Rosewood, banana, and applewoods. Spindle turning. The tall shape results when each turning is left attached. The small shapes, below, result when the individual turned forms are separated as in the bead demonstration following.

A piece of wood is roughed with the roundnose.

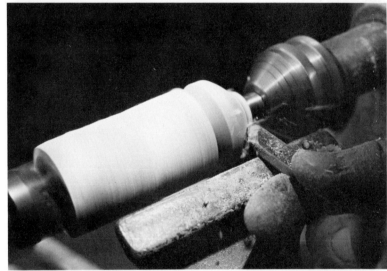

The wood is roughed into a round and one of the beads is beginning to be shaped.

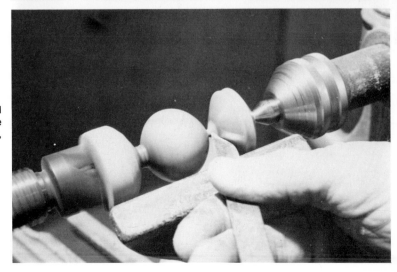

Shaping is done with an elongated skew to cut deeply between the beads. Two beads are being turned, each will be 1 inch in diameter.

The beads are sanded on the lathe with a series of papers from coarse to fine until the bead is as smooth as desired.

An oil finish is rubbed on with the cloth. If a varnish or lacquer is desired, it can be applied in the same way.

The beads are cut apart with a saw.

Holes for stringing are drilled.

*Opposite:* A string of finished wooden beads of different sizes, shapes, and woods combined with amber. By Lawrence B. Hunter.

*Above:* Footed serving dish by Bob Higbee made of two pieces of black walnut. 6″ high, 11″ diameter.

*Left:* An assortment of small weed pots by Bob Higbee. Six-inch diameters of dried slabs of different woods retain the shape of the log and some bark for texture. Woods include Australian teak, mesquite, apple, cork oak, manzanita. Each is about 3 1/2″ high. Only the tops and bottoms are cut during turning. The pots are sealed with polyurethane and wax.

*Above:* Chess set and box by Tripp Carpenter. Turned chess pieces are quayacau and bay burl. The box is 5" square, and made of quayacau and rosewood.

*Below:* By Ada Dally. Turned cup and saucer with hand-carved cup handle. Highly figured New Zealand knitia-excelsa wood. Cup 3" high, 2 3/4" diameter. Saucer 5 1/2" diameter.

*Courtesy, artist*

*Right:* Vase by Tripp Carpenter combines an ebony wood top with an ivory base—both turned on the lathe. 4" high, 2" diameter.

*Above:* A pair of cleft vases by Mel Mordaunt with insets of contrasting colored and textured woods. Turned and hand-carved teak and padouk. 5″ high, 4″ diameter.

*Courtesy, artist*

*Below:* By Euripides Toro. A lathe-turned custom-designed stand to hold bangle bracelets. Walnut. The carved base is approximately 15″ wide, 13″ deep, the turnings range from 6 1/2″ to 10″ high.

*Above:* Vase by Bob Higbee. Olive and black walnut. 3 1/2'' high, 2'' diameter.

*Above right:* Wooden weed pot by Robert Cumpston. 11'' high, 6'' diameter. All of Mr. Cumpston's pots are made from fence posts or telephone and utility poles that are old and weathered enough for the creosote to have bled out of them. After turning, they are lightly burned with a propane and special torch tip, then cleaned on a wire wheel and polished.

*Right:* By Euripides Toro. Turned container of oak with a black walnut base and hand-carved animal antler lid. 4 1/2'' high, 3 1/2'' diameter.

*Far right:* Candle holder by John Bickel. Brazilian rosewood. 8 1/4'' high, 3 1/4'' base diameter. The base and top are turned; the center section is hand carved all from one piece of wood.

*Courtesy, artist*

## STEPHEN HOGBIN'S OVERSIZED TURNINGS

There is more than one way to turn a piece of wood using the lathe concept. Stephen Hogbin, dismayed by the size limitations of a turning on a conventional lathe, devised a turning device that would accommodate wood as large as five feet in diameter, and maybe more. The application of this turning method is only beginning to be explored by Mr. Hogbin and those who have already been stimulated and inspired by him.

Hogbin's experiments began with the usual lathe turnings, and then the concept of cutting apart the round resulted. But cutting apart a 12-inch turning only resulted in 4-by-4-inch pieces that weren't too practical. Hogbin expanded the concept and gradually visualized new ways to turn and apply the wood to art form. Mr. Hogbin realized that turnings larger than the usual board width could be accomplished only by edge gluing. He first laminated boards to one another to create a larger circumference for a turning. Then he laminated the pieces with a piece of cardboard between the edges so the turnings could be shaped, then be cut apart again and reassembled in myriad combinations. These reassemblies could be used for sculpture, for complete pieces of furniture such as tables, chairs, and so forth, and they could also be applied to objects as decorative, geometrical yet asymmetrical designs. If the sandwiched cardboard was preshaped and the wood cut down to the design, it could also serve as a template for the turning.

The result is an ability to make round turnings, cut them apart, and have them yield rectangular bowls, oblique and other shapes first unexpected, then well-planned.

The mechanics of building the unit are offered by Mr. Hogbin in the drawing on page 97. The breakdown of the differential mechanism is also given.

Basically, the wood-turning device is made from salvaged pipe, a truck's rear axle and differential turned by a one horsepower motor. Using the basic approach, one can create a similar device that is adaptable to any individual forms visualized by the woodworker.

A block of wood made of two boards has been laminated across the center with a piece of cardboard glued between (*left*). It is attached to the faceplate of the lathe, made from pipe and a truck motor. Turning proceeds in the usual faceplate scraping procedure.

After the object has been turned, it is split on the cardboard line using a wedge or mallet and chisel.

*Demonstration: Stephen Hogbin*
*Photos, author*

If desired, the board can again be fragmented into other shapes which can be applied to box tops, furniture, mirror edges, and so forth. The demonstration is with a small piece of wood, but the use of larger diameters offers additional points of departure for experimenting with the forms on a grander scale.

*Top:* Salad bowl, by Stephen Hogbin, of laminated woods turned and divided from a larger form.

*Center:* A pair of bowls by Stephen Hogbin showing the inside and outside, lathe turned and cut from a larger turning. Maple, 10″ diameter.

*Left:* Maple salad bowl by Stephen Hogbin. 10″ diameter.

¾ TON AXLE AND DIFFERENTIAL (FORD)
SLOWEST SPEED 60 RPM
TOP SPEED APPROX 1000 RPM
WELD GEARS OR FIX ONE
END FOR POWER INPUT

2" to 17½" DIA V BELT
3" to 13" DIA PULLEY
4" to 8" DIA
5 to 5½" DIA
— 4 DIA

AXLE

HEADSTOCK
SPINDLE

FACE PLATE

AXLE

TAIL STOCK
SPINDLE
AXLE RUNS
FREE

FREE STANDING
TAIL STOCK

JACK POST
TO CEILING

REMOVE FOR
FACE PLATE WORK

INDEX PIN

FACE PLATE

BUFFING
WHEEL
SANDING
DISK

AXLE CUT
IN HALF

TABLE WITH
DRAWERS

TOOL REST

SWITCH

MOTOR
HANGS ON
V BELT

1 HORSE
MOTOR

TO POWER
SOURCE

1" DIA
PIPE

44½"

BOLT TO
FLOOR

2" DIA
PIPE

44"

1" DIA
PIPE

CENTRE 44½" HIGH
HEAD STOCK 44" x 63" PLAN
TAIL STOCK 33" x 30" PLAN

2" DIA
PIPE

17½"

Drawing of the lathe made from pipe and
a truck motor . . .

. . . with a detail of differential assembly.
*Courtesy, Stephen Hogbin*

PULLEY

BUFFING
WHEEL

DIFFERENTIAL

# 4 The Laminated Object

*Opposite top:* Weed bottles by William Jaquith Evans. A variety of laminated woods hand carved, approximately 6″ high.

*Opposite below:* By William Jaquith Evans. Multilaminates in several directions are made into a box with laminated screw peg fasteners. 4″ high, 10 1/2″ wide, 4 1/2″ deep.

*Above:* Jewelry box by Charles M. Kaplan. Three laminated layers using walnut sandwiched between cherry. Hand carved. Two sliding drawers are neatly finished so they are barely visible when the box is closed. 7″ high, 12″ wide.

*Courtesy, artist*

The process of building up the surface dimension of wood by layering is called laminating. It has been accomplished by woodworkers for centuries. Until the invention of glues in the middle 1700s, all laminates were dry joined. Today the application and holding power of modern adhesives makes laminating more efficient and practical than ever. Many object makers rely heavily on the use of laminating procedures for much of their work, whether it is by lathe turning, direct carving, constructing, or combinations of all techniques. They use laminating to combine different colors and textures of wood to result in a finished item with a visual and tactile appearance that is not possible using only one kind. They also laminate to yield a block of wood larger than a single board thickness.

Technically, the process of laminating involves layering two or more pieces of wood in any desired manner, either by placing the board surfaces next to each other, by gluing edges in different arrangements, by combining edge and board surfaces, or by inserting veneers between the laminates. It is also feasible to sandwich in other materials such as clear and colored sheets of acrylic and metals using adhesives that are compatible to all surfaces.

The surfaces to be laminated must be planed flat so that no gaps occur between the layers. The movement of the board's grains should be considered for expansion and shrinkage; coarse-grain woods used in damp climates, for example, may tend to separate at the glue lines. It is always good practice to assemble the boards and clamp them first without gluing to ascertain the smoothness of the surfaces and to eliminate any possible gaps. When you are satisfied with the dry clamping, then glue the surfaces and clamp adequately all around the pieces. Allow to dry thoroughly before working. Once dry, the laminates can be handled the same as a solid block of wood. Refer to the glue listing (pages 34-39) for glues available and their properties. If you plan to do quantity laminates with any given set of woods, it is wise to glue up samples using different glues to determine which give the most satisfactory results for your purposes.

Prelaminated woods of birch, plywood, and others are available from lumber dealers. These are thin layers of wood that have been glued cross-grained to one another and prepared as board for a variety of woodworking procedures. One can use the laminated boards as they are, or combine several layers for a thicker working dimension. They are also interesting when the prelaminated boards are layered in with other woods such as mahogany or walnut for differences in thickness of layers and coloration.

A variety of laminating ideas will be found in this chapter and throughout the book. They are as simple and effective as the three-layer bowls made by Charles Kaplan and as complex and jigsaw puzzlelike as the vases and other items made by William Jaquith Evans. Will Evans often uses his intricate laminates as veneers. After building up a block of various woods he will slice them veneer thin and place these veneers over a piece of inexpensive wood. With this procedure he achieves different patterns on every surface of the box and no two boxes are exactly alike because he can alter the direction of the veneer. The combinations are infinite, the procedure imaginative.

Paul Kopel develops his laminated forms by another technique. The shape is first developed in a clay model, then transposed to a laminated block of plastic foam. The foam is carved to shape and sliced the thickness of the boards to be laminated. Each slice is outlined on a board which is cut to shape. The preshaped boards are glued and clamped, resulting in a sculptural form that needs only final shaping, sanding, and finishing. This procedure permits the artist to develop sculptural form by adding on and/or carving the clay to achieve his design in the same way the sculptor works. Normally, woodworking becomes a subtractive process by which the form is attained by carving. If you carve away too much, the original form envisioned must be altered to accommodate any errors. Mr. Kopel demonstrates the procedure in the series on pages 108-111.

The procedure for building up a laminated block is demonstrated by Lawrence B. Hunter. The laminate can consist of different thicknesses of wood. A board is sliced in half on a band saw. The edges and surfaces should be put on a planer—to make them perfectly flat so they will adhere to the adjacent layers—and then sanded smooth on a belt sander.

The layers are "tested" for fit and coloration. Layers of angelique and light Philippine mahogany are interspersed with maple veneers. Dry clamp for close fit and be sure you have enough clamps.

Spread glue on the layers.

Clamp up the boards. When the glue oozes, it's a good sign that the joints fit tightly. Drying time will depend on the type of glue used.

When the laminate is dry, you can cut any
shape you like to achieve effects similar to
those in the boxes by William Jaquith Evans.

You could then insert another veneer in this
way and reclamp.

You can make as many cuts as you like to
yield different shapes and laminate patterns.

Another cut reveals new possibilities.

You could place one set of cut laminates on the other and reglue and clamp. Then slice and use the slices for the surface of an object.

You can assemble the parts in any way. This could be a box if a backing and a cover were assembled to it. It could be the framed box for a mirror set onto the back and covered with another layer of wood or with laminated layers. The potentials are infinite once you begin playing with the woods and visualizing new forms.

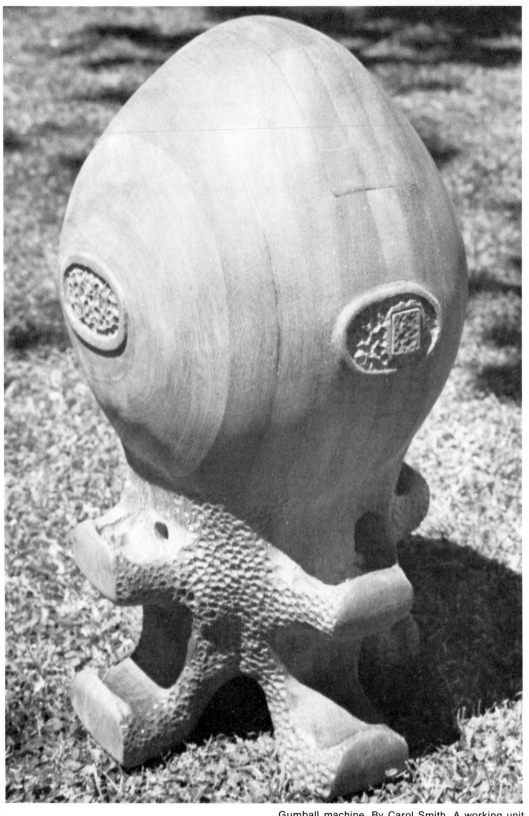

Gumball machine. By Carol Smith. A working unit of laminated woods. A removable panel at right can be filled with gumballs. The square wood "button" is pushed in to release the balls, which fall through to four holes and troughs around the machine.

*Photo, Lawrence B. Hunter*

Front and back views of laminated boxes with mirrors inset. By William Jaquith Evans. The intricate patterning is accomplished by end and face laying-in of narrow and wide laminates. Sizes are approximately 5″ and 6 1/2″ high, by 2″ and 3″ wide and deep.

*Top:* Weed holder or vase by Charles M. Kaplan. Stripes are veneers laminated between walnut boards. 16'' high.

*Courtesy, artist*

*Below:* Breadboard by Wayne Raab. Cherry and maple. 12'' long, 9'' wide. Curved cuts have veneers laminated between the curves.

*Right:* By William Jaquith Evans. Laminated teak cabinet with locking devices. Cabinet holds a sterling silver bud vase cast from one of the artist's own laminated wood vases. 11 1/2" high, 5 1/2" wide, 5" deep.

*Below:* By Espenet. Redwood burl drawer fronts in a laminated walnut case. Drawers (*right*) are cut out with a band saw which provides a kerf the exact thickness of the felt lining used in and around the drawer interiors. 22" high, 4" wide, 5" deep.

## PROCEDURE FOR LAMINATING FROM A FOAM MODEL
by PAUL S. KOPEL

*Left:* A drawing and clay model of a clock base show the beginning steps in Paul's work-up. Two-inch-thick foam blocks will be used for the laminate patterns. Foam slabs come in different thicknesses 1, 2, and 3″ and in large slabs 2′ X 8′ which are cut to sizes necessary for the block.

*Below:* The clock in plastic foam is shown after the form has been carved from the foam blocks. Tools used for shaping the foam are knives, a Surform rasp, chisels, and a hot wire for slicing the foam.

*Above:* The foam sections when separated: the inside has been hollowed out. Holes were drilled for registering and holding the slices together but these did not work as they were too close to the outer carved surfaces.

*Left:* The 2-inch-thick foam pieces are laminated by gluing with white glue or contact cement. They must dry for about a week so the glue will cure. They are shaped, then sliced to board thickness with a hot wire.

*Right:* The cutout wood laminates are glued.

*Below:* The shape of each foam piece is traced onto a board and numbered.

*Above:* One half of the form is glued and clamped at one time. Later, both halves will be clamped together.

*Above right:* The inside shape that will hold the clock mechanism is carved out with hand chisels. A piece of wood remains for attaching the clock to the jig, which holds the face horizontal and rotates it in a circular manner under the router bit in the drill press.

A bottom view shows both halves clamped together and the cutout that will hold the clock's mechanism.

Shaping continues with a gouge and a variety of hand tools.

A drawknife helps round off edges quickly.

A Surform rasp continues the smoothing process.

The clockface is shaped with a router attachment on a drill press.

A jig holds the clock in the drill press so it can be rotated horizontally.

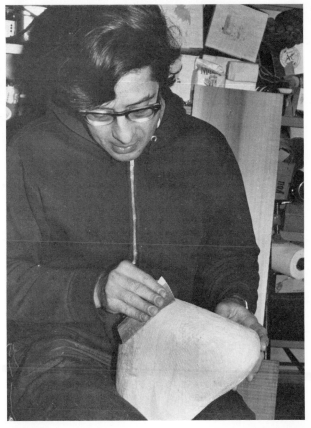

The clock as it appears before final finishing. The clockface and mechanism may be purchased ready-made.

Paul finishes the piece by hand, using several grades of sanding materials. See the following page for the finished piece.

*Demonstration by Paul S. Kopel*
*Photos by Sally K. Davidson*

Clock by Paul S. Kopel. The face is laminated cherry and walnut with brass hour marks.
11″ high, 13″ wide, 8″ deep. Shap-
ing for all objects has been with the plastic-
foam layering technique shown in the previous series.
*Collection, Dr. and Mrs. Donald Tucker*
*Rochester, New York*
*Photo, Campbell Studio*

Standing mirror by Paul S. Kopel. laminated Honduras mahogany. 24'' high, 12'' diameter.

*Photo, Campbell Studio*

By Paul S. Kopel. Bowl of laminated Finnish birch plywood. 5'' high, 12'' wide, 6'' deep.

*Collection, Mr. and Mrs. Trevor Ewell*
*Rochester, New York*
*Photo, Campbell Studio*

# The Carved Object

*Above:* By Lawrence R. Jones. A laminated box with pivoting lid of East Indian rosewood, padouk, ebony, and zebrawood.

*Courtesy, artist*

*Right:* By Frank E. Cummings III. A container, lathe turned and hand carved. East Indian rosewood with buffalo fur and goat. Horsehair coiled basketry detail is on the lid. 12″ high, 7″ diameter.

*Opposite:* Deer with Antlers. By Joe Nyiri. A hat rack of hand-carved mahogany with animal horn antlers. Approximately 20″ high.

115

Since primitive man first shaped tools and weapons from wood, the idea of carving and shaping wood for useful objects has been part of every culture. Primitive man was interested only in the form as it would function; today's object makers are interested in the form as both function and sculpture. This dual love affair with the potential of wood is apparent in the multitude and variety of examples in the following pages.

Coupled with this near-romantic involvement with wood is the sentiment that many craftsmen have about the material itself; they like to handle it, turn it, carve it, and watch the form evolve slowly, using mostly hand tools for the creative portions and power tools for roughing and finishing procedures. The forms are not those that can be achieved solely by mechanical tools; they are often free forms, organic shapes, textures, and movements that are essentially in the realm of hand-driven tools such as chisels, gouges, rasps, and files.

A great many carvers prefer to work from a log and work only from logs they themselves have found, cut, and cured. Others may be equally happy evolving their forms from cut boards, from laminated blocks, or from either logs or boards.

The ambivalent attitudes underscore the fact that there is no one way to develop a wood object. Nor does one have to be a purist. The tools used by Mexican artist José Margaro Quiroz's practiced hand are driven with utmost control and a desire for a decorative linear quality. The wood blank that is deftly carved into a bowl with a chain saw and finished with power tools by Jocko Johnson has an elegant shape, subtle curves, and beautiful finish.

The containers by Frank E. Cummings III combine hand carving with the jewelers' techniques and tools. His exciting examples utilize wood in combination with silver and ivory inlays, copper enameling, bone, horn, shells, bristles, jute, and other materials.

Jim Traynor's bottles are made from two pieces of wood glued together. First, he hollows the interior shape out of each half using a template and hand tools, so the bottle walls will be 3/8 to 1/2 inch thick. Then two halves are glued together, dried, and the exterior shape turned on a lathe. The bottles are lighter weight than if only a hole were bored through the center. The interiors are coated with several layers of sealer so they can be used as a bottle and so the object fulfills the purpose of a container.

Each artist strives to develop a design concept that is original. It may be purely imaginative or it may be derived from a source that interests him: organic, architectural, fanciful, or from the inspiration of primitive and early cultures. Once the function of the piece is established, the design is envisioned, and the work proceeds from rough sketches, detailed drawings, or the imagination. But that doesn't mean it all evolves without any problems. Given the multitude of nature's changes that permeate a piece of wood at different points in the tree's life, such as knotholes, checks and rays, summer and winter growth, and insect infiltration, the carver may have to change his direction. Larry Hunter was working with a walnut log that he had cured for two years. He had a bowl planned for the piece that would combine lathe turning and hand carving. Once he cut away the bark, a series of soft, spongy areas within the wood made it impossible to turn without chipping out large splinters. That log eventually became a beautiful hand-carved bowl with unusual shaping and texturing that he developed around the imperfections in the log.

*Opposite left top:* An early American food grinder meant to be only functional has sculptural qualities in its total designs as well as in the individual parts. 20″ high, 12″ diameter.

*Opposite left center:* A turban holder from Afghanistan with intricate hand carvings. 25″ high, 17″ diameter.

*Opposite left below:* A wood *garudha* from Bali has a back that opens and is a container. 12″ high, 15″ diameter.

*Opposite right top:* A carved wood support for a pole that holds an instrument in the Balinese orchestra. 12″ high, 6″ diameter.

*Opposite right below:* Wood mortar and pestle from Afghanistan is hand carved with carved surface decorations.

*All objects, collection
Mr. and Mrs. W. Chapman
Solana Beach, California*

## TOOLS

The kinds of tools available for direct carving are wide and varied. The basic cutting tools are knives, chisels, gouges, and rasps—with variations in sizes and shapes. A mallet of hardwood, usually lignum vitae, is used to drive the tool into the wood. Depending upon the size of the piece of wood you are working with, a holding device may be required. C-clamps, wood clamps, vises, and any improvised setup may be used to anchor the wood to a bench or other working surface. Primitive carvers often hold the wood with their bare feet, but unless you want to lose a few toes, this is not recommended. Sculpture supply houses and woodworker suppliers' catalogs should be studied for any equipment that might work well for your purpose. Odd-shaped pieces of wood may be tied to a log or anvil for anchoring as you work.

Gouges and chisels are designed with cutting edges of different shapes and widths including straight edges, V-shapes graduating to a spoon shape, and some with tapered, fine-pointed blades. They are classed in three ways:

a) shape—straight, curved, or bent
b) width—at the cutting edge in inches or millimeters
c) section—the shape at the cutting edge.

A code number is usually stamped on the shaft. Catalogs of woodworking tools list approximately 400 available types of blades. Lines simulate the shape of the cutting edges available.

Purchasing the best tools you can afford is the greatest economy in the long run. A good tool, made of high quality tempered steel, holds a sharp edge and can be resharpened many times. Handles can be replaced if they break under the blow of the mallet. Some craftsmen prefer to make shaped and weighted handles to their own specifications, so it is possible to purchase blades separately.

An assortment of rasps, files, and scrapers are used for blending large areas and smoothing surfaces, particularly in hardwoods that will be further sandpapered and polished. Files tend to leave deep marks in softwoods. Rasps and files are made in flat, round, half-round, and other shapes.

Rifflers are small files and rasps that are curved and tapered at each end. They are used for working into awkward corners and rounded areas.

The usual carpenters' tools, an essential part of the craftsman's workshop, are used in combination with sculptors' tools. There also may be tools you are not familiar with, and regular forays through tool catalogs and into hardware departments of local stores can yield surprises. You may have overlooked certain tools because the need for them hadn't arisen. As you encounter problems, you may find easy solutions for them.

Direct carving can certainly be accomplished with many power tools, too. The combination of hand tools and power tools should be employed to facilitate any aspect of the work.

## SHARPENING HAND CARVING TOOLS

Woodcutting tools dull and nick quickly and have to be resharpened frequently. In some areas, tools can be taken to professional sharpeners, but the self-sufficient craftsman usually prefers to sharpen them himself, when he needs them. To hand sharpen, the tool is rubbed on an oilstone. Oilstones are made in straight and curved shapes to fit the differently shaped tools. The blade is passed along the stone according to the angle of the blade and the defect to be remedied. A woodcutting chisel is beveled on one edge only, but both edges must be sharp, so the tool is passed along the stone in one direction until the necessary angle and degree of sharpness are achieved. It is reversed frequently from front to back as it is worked.

A mechanical grinding stone will sharpen a blade in about an eighth of the time required with oilstones. Generally, the sharpening procedure is as follows:

1. Rough-sharpen or grind the tool until the defect or blunt edge is gone and a heavy burr appears. When using a grinding wheel, be especially careful not to "burn" the edge by letting it become hot which causes the tool to lose temper. Constantly dip the tool in oil or cold water to cool it.

2. Sharpening then becomes a process of carefully working the stone back and forth over both sides of the edge until the burr is totally removed. It falls off like a thin curly hair.

3. There are many ways to hold and work the stone and tool when removing the burr. Practice and experience are required before you find the technique that is best for you.

Test the sharpness of a blade by cutting across the grain of a piece of pinewood. A tool may seem to be cutting clean in hardwood, but when it is tested on soft pine, defects in the cutting edge can be detected more quickly. When testing blades, do not hold the wood in the one hand in front of the tool and the tool in the other. A very sharp tool may easily slip off the wood and cut your hand. Always keep both hands behind the cutting edge of the tool when testing, sharpening, and working. Never try to catch a falling tool. Wear safety glasses or goggles to avoid particles and dust from getting into the eyes.

Small wood stool made by the Ashanti of Africa. 10" high, 24" wide.
*Collection, Mr. and Mrs. W. Chapman*
*Solana Beach, California*

Assorted carver's tools include gouges with differently shaped blade edges, a lignum vitae mallet, hammer, and chisels with blades of varying widths and angles of cutting edge.

There are approximately 400 differently shaped gouges and chisels available. A few basic curved and V cutting edges are shown above with the type of cut they make.

Curved and straight blade and chip-carving knives are excellent for cutting into soft woods.

Flat, round, and half-round rasps and rifflers and assorted shaped Surfoam tools are used for blending large areas and smoothing surfaces.

Welcome additions to a carver's workbox might be a folding-handle drawknife, an adz, spokeshave, and a slick. The slick, used in shipbuilding, is a large flat chisel ideal for flattening mortise surfaces or other areas which cannot be planed.

The hand tool should be sharpened on an oilstone (two types are shown). Stones are made in various sizes, types, and shapes to fit differently shaped tools. The blade is passed along the stone according to the angle of the blade and the defect is remedied. The burr is removed by honing. The sharpness of a blade is tested by cutting across the grain of a piece of pine.

Hand-carving procedures have changed little since the first tools were used to chip wood and the techniques are the same in every culture. Mr. José Margaro Quiroz, a master wood-carver from Mexico, demonstrates how quickly a skilled hand can manipulate razor sharp gouges and chisels to create sculptural design in the edge of a piece of hardwood. The tools are driven by both calloused hand and mallet. The wood is mahogany, but the artist carves so quickly that one would think he was cutting into butter.

*Photographed at the woodworking shop*
*of the Muñoz Furniture Factory,*
*Tijuana, Mexico*
*Photos, author*

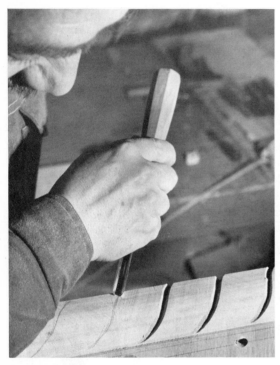

He cuts a deep curving line with a V-shaped gouge . . .

. . . and continues to widen it near the top.

He cuts into the groove with a rounded chisel . . .

. . . and works up into the center of the groove with a flat chisel.

Another groove is made at about a 45° angle to the first one.

He uses the side of the hammer to drive the chisel and penetrate the wood with a sharp, quick, slightly curved cut.

A broad-blade curved chisel smooths off the layers.

He continues to bring out the curved linear shape . . .

. . . and gives the sweeping design a final staccato note with a sharp V gouge.

There is a wide selection of small power tools available to do myriad carving jobs from hairline cuts to deep gouges. Many of the versatile units have a variety of attachments. *Above:* the basic Unimat Miniature Machine is outfitted with a flexible shaft to power a hand drill.

*Courtesy, American Edelstaal, Inc.*
*Tenafly, New Jersey*

A complete all-family home workshop that operates as a jigsaw, disk sander, buffing wheel, grinder, and flexible shaft is offered by Dremel.

*Courtesy, Dremel Mfg. Co.*
*Racine, Wisconsin*

Dremel also has a hand-held variable-speed Moto-tool for a variety of carving needs, with innumerable shaped bits for working in wood, metal, plastic, bone, stone, and other materials.

Redwood garden wall. By Bennett Wade.
60'' high, 42'' wide.

*Courtesy, artist*

Ritual Object by Lisa Dahilen Dorfer. Wood
with brush. 38'' high, 29'' wide.

## ROUGH CUTTING WITH A CHAIN SAW

There are several ways to rough out a blank of wood to start a bowl or other shape using direct carving methods. The usual procedure is to chip away with wide gouges until the rough shape evolves, and then proceed to refine the shape and finish with hand and power tools. One can also drill into a blank and then chip away the remaining parts of the wood with hand tools. But Jocko Johnson finds that the use of a chain saw is, with a little practice, a quick and efficient way to hollow out the bowl.

The block is first cut to exterior shaping with a band saw. The tip of the chain saw blade is used to cut grooves which are crosscut and chipped out. Further finishing is accomplished with a rotary sanding disk placed in the drill head using an improvised valve seat grinder and working from 36 to 120 to 320 grit paper. Shaping is also done with various bits in a flexible shaft.

Jocko often fills in a hole that remains in the wood with a gemstone, using epoxy or acrylic resin to hold it in place and sanding the stone flush with the wood surface and polishing it.

Below, the evolution from pieces of rough-sawn walnut to the finished bowls are shown. Each bowl can be created in a few hours with this procedure which Jocko demonstrates in the following series.

The walnut blank is positioned against a supporting piece of wood, which Jocko stands on to steady.

Carving into the block begins with the tip of the gas-powered chain saw. A series of parallel lines about 3/4 of the thickness of the wood is cut across the blank.

Once all the horizontals are cut, crosscuts are made to begin chipping out the wood.

These cuts and the roughing were accomplished in about five minutes.

With the block still propped against the supporting wood, the last fragments of the interior waste wood are removed.

The shape is further refined with a sanding disk backed by a rubber pad and placed in a high speed grinder (1300 RPM).

The flexibility enables Jocko to move the sander up the gradual sloping of the bowl sides.

Grind-O-Flex sander on a Dumore flexible shaft grinder is used for additional smoothing.

Seated comfortably in a beanbag chair with the essential-to-wear face mask, Jocko begins to shape the bottom of the bowl with a series of different large bits normally used for grinding metals in automotive work.

He uses different shaped bits for taking down the lip and side.

A ball-shaped rotary file in the flexible shaft makes the indented area below the lip.

The finished walnut bowl by Jocko Johnson is 2" high, 12" wide and 3 1/2" deep.

*Demonstration, Jocko Johnson*
*Photos, author*

By Keith E. Stephens. Hand-carved black walnut tray. 2″ high, 24″ wide, 12″ deep. *Below*, hand-carved bowl. By Robert Tront.

*Courtesy, artist*

By J. B. Blunk. Salad bowl. Walnut. 8″ high, 14″ wide, 16″ deep. Rough gouge marks become the decorative detailing of the object which has a different form on each side. Three views.

*Above:* By Lyle Laske. A teak vessel, 10 1/4''
high, 31'' wide, 13'' deep.
*Collection, Francine Laske*
*Courtesy, artist*

*Center:* By Dan L. Valenza. Myrtlewood.
3 1/2'' high, 17'' wide, 5'' deep.
*Photo, artist*

*Below:* Handled tray by Dan L. Valenza. Walnut. 17'' wide, 15'' deep.
*Photo, artist*

*Above:* By Hal E. Davis. A black walnut box designed around the figuring from the tree crotch used in the lid (*closed*).

*Courtesy, artist*

*Below:* By Patricia Spalding. Walnut. 2″ high, 13″ wide, 9″ deep.

*Photo, Dan L. Valenza*

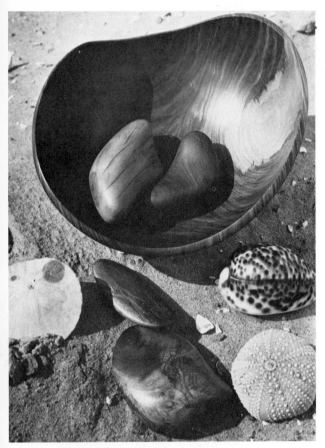

*Left:* By Jim Traynor. Lignum vitae bowl 5″ high, 9″ diameter with free-form-shaped "feelies" of different types of wood.

*Below left:* By Tom Taylor. Compartmented dish of desert ironwood with a centerpiece of mahonia wood and a variety of dot inlays. 1 1/2″ high, 4 1/2″ wide, 3 1/4″ deep.

*Below center:* By J. B. Blunk. A bowl made of drift redwood, taking advantage of the natural texture for the exterior with carved and finished interior. Limpet seashells added on. 2″ high, 21″ wide, 6″ deep.

*Above:* By Leroy Hogue. Walnut dishes for crackers and mints: cracker dish, *front*, 1 5/8", 24" wide, 2 1/2" deep. Mint dish, *rear*, 2" high, 8 1/4" wide, 4 1/2" deep.
*Courtesy, artist*

*Center and below:* Two bowls hand carved by Ann Malmlund from circles of cured logs. Top, 3" high, 18" diameter. *Below:* Check has been corrected by the decorative addition of an inset piece of wood, 3" high, 22" diameter.

*Above:* Kitchen utensils by Robert Lehman. Hand- and machine-carved red oak. Overall 1/2 inch thick, 20'' high, 15'' wide.

*Center:* Cutting board by John Bauer of two boards, edge laminated, then carved by machine and hand in shape of bull. Maple body with eyes and nose of inlaid partridgewood. 1 1/2'' thick, 25'' long, 15'' wide.

*Below:* Dog-shaped cutting board by John Bauer. Genessera wood, eyes inlaid of purpleheart, ebony, and ramon wood. 2'' thick, 19'' wide, 15'' deep.

*From top to bottom:* By Peter Boiger. Black walnut cutting board 3 1/2" high, 17 1/2" wide, 9" deep. Chopper of ebony, handles with silver pegs and a stainless steel blade. 5" high, 8 1/2" wide.

Meat block. By Dan L. Valenza. Walnut. 5" high, 22" wide, 13" deep.

*Photo, artist*

Tray/cutting board by J. B. Blunk made from a redwood burl. 3" high, 16" wide, 7" deep.

Cheeseboard by Tom Bendon. Laminated black walnut and zebrawood. 10" wide, approximately 5" deep.

*Courtesy, Design 11*
*ACC South Central Region*

By Dan L. Valenza. Tray. Walnut. 22'' diameter.

*Photo, artist*

Tray, *front and back views*. By J. B. Blunk, Madrone. 2'' high, 17'' wide, 10'' deep.

*Top:* Hand-carved teak bowl. By Keith E. Stephens. 2" high, 18" wide, 7" deep.
*Collection, Mr. and Mrs. W. Chapman Solana Beach, California*

*Center left:* Covered dish. By Lawrence B. Hunter. Teak with acrylic plastic. Ten-inch hand-carved knife handle. Acrylic dome cover is blown with air pressure after acrylic has been softened in an oven.

*Center right:* Tray. By Jere Osgood. Brazilian rosewood. 2" high, 18" wide, 11" deep.
*Courtesy, artist*

*Below:* Tray. By Keith E. Stephens. Teak with contrasting circle inlays. 2" high, 23" wide, 8 1/2" deep.

*Opposite:* By Peter Boiger. Hand-carved salad servers of ebony, Brazilian rosewood, Indian rosewood, and walnut ranging from 12″ to 16″ long.

*Left below:* By Stephen Hogbin. Cherry wood salad servers. 12″ and 13″ long. They are designed with a lip that hooks on edge of bowl to keep them from sliding in. They may also be stored hanging on the edge of shelf as a decorative item. Maple salad bowl. 10-inch diameter.

*Right below:* Cherry wood ladle. Two views. By Stephen Hogbin. 13″ long.

*Above:* By Lawrence B. Hunter. *Left to right,* Rosewood spoon 14″ long. Rosewood spatula 9″ long, teak spoon 9″ long, brass and teak ladle 7″ long, avocado bowl 5″ diameter.

*Center:* By Ed Zucca. Cherrywood scoop. 10″ long, 7″ wide.

*Courtesy, artist*

*Below:* By Don Boyd. Soup ladle of hand-carved applewood. 12″ long. Flour scoop of hand-carved applewood, 7″ long.

*Above left:* By Jay O'Rourke. Spoon and fork with heart-shape handle tip. Goncalo alves. 7 1/2″ long, 1 1/2″ wide.

*Below left:* By Stephen R. Johnson. Spatulas and butter spreader of shedua. Spatulas are 12″ long, 3″ wide. Spreader is 8″ long, 1 1/4″ wide.

*Top right:* By Jocko Johnson. Spurtle (spoon-paddle). Black walnut. 14″ long, 2 1/2″ wide.

*Center right:* By Dan L. Valenza. Bowl with spreader. Walnut. 3″ high, 11″ square.

*Photo, artist*

*Below right:* By Mel Mordaunt. Butter dish. Teak with acrylic. 3 1/4″ high, 4 1/2″ wide, 2 3/4″ deep.

*Above:* By Frank E. Cummings III. Hand-carved container of ebony with horsehair and ermine fur. 9″ high, 9″ wide, 7″ deep.

*Opposite top left:* By Frank E. Cummings III. Covered container of East Indian rosewood with Mylar insets, ermine fur, and quail feathers. 6 1/2″ high, 3 1/2″ diameter.

*Top right:* By Frank E. Cummings III. Footed, covered container of ebony with ivory inlay around foot and dentalium shells with hackle feathers. 8″ high, 3″ diameter.

*Opposite below left:* By Frank E. Cummings III. Ebony with ivory, hackle feathers. 5″ high, 3 1/2″ diameter.

*Opposite below right:* By Frank E. Cummings III. Ivory container with an ebony lid and base. Ivory inlaid around neck of lid. Gold-tipped hackle feathers around crown pick up gold color pegging in ivory. Frank works many of the details with jeweler's tools.

*Above:* By Jocko Johnson. Ironwood covered containers are hand carved from a roughed-out blank (*center*) and shown partially completed in foreground and fully finished in background. Detail shows interior and finish of inner lid with a piece of cork and a round of wood to keep cover from sliding.

*Below left:* A student at California State University, Long Beach, hand carved a hanging container with flowing lines that echo the grain of the wood.

*Right:* Another Long Beach student created a formed leather container with a hand-carved neckpiece.

*Above:* By Bob Falwell. A walnut box (*closed and open views*) 6″ high, 7″ wide, 7″ deep.

*Above left and center:* By Sterling King. A covered container with a hand-carved hinged top that lifts to reveal a leather-covered interior.
*Photographed at Triforium Galleries, San Diego, California*

*Below left:* By Lawrence B. Hunter. Walnut container with brass fitting and silver skeleton jewelry piece inside. 15″ high, 6″ wide, 5 1/2″ deep.

By Michael Graham. A "McCallister box" of
African rosewood and Brazilian pau ferro.
18" high, 12" wide, 12" deep.
*Courtesy, artist*

*Left:* Jewel container by Frank E. Cummings III. Brazilian rosewood and black hackle feathers. 12″ high, 6″ diameter.

*Below left:* By Lawrence R. Jones. The covered container is made of lathe-turned laminated padouk with hand-carved legs and trim of East Indian rosewood. 5 1/2″ high.
*Courtesy, artist*

*Below right:* Jewelry box by Espenet. Holly with ebony knobs. 20″ high, 4″ wide, 5″ deep.
*Courtesy, artist*

Zebrawood jewel box by Hal E. Davis (*open and closed*). There are three drawer compartments, two lidded compartments, and one pivoting double compartment. 6" high, 18" wide, 12" deep.

*Courtesy, artist*

*Above:* By Fundi Kiburi. Jewel box (*closed and open*). Amaranth and zebrawood with a cocobolo catch. Compartments in lid are held closed by carved ivory turn buttons. There is an ivory inlay in the elephant's eye in front carving. Box bottom is dark glass.
*Collection, Mel Mordaunt*

*Below:* By Hal E. Davis. Figured maple jewel box with five drawers and one lidded compartment. Approximately 6″ high, 18″ wide, 12″ deep. Open and closed views. Drawers pull out with elongated handles.
*Courtesy, artist*

*Left:* By Dan L. Valenza. Piggy I jewelry chest. Laminated walnut lined in red velvet. Says Dan, "I began producing these designs as a lark and eventually was caught up in the theme: producing an amusing, if not indeed a ridiculous form, useful and perhaps a bit satirical in its stated use." The drawers have a compression in workings that produces a suck and whoosh as they are opened and shut. 6" high, 12" wide, 15" deep.

*Photo, artist*

*Below left:* Chest of East Indian rosewood by Tom Tramel. 36" high, 22" wide, 16" deep.

*Photo, artist*

*Below right:* Jewel box. By Espenet. Guatemalan gavalea wood. 24" high, 6" wide, 4" deep. Drawers pull from the front and side.

TABLE SETTING. By Jim Traynor. Lathe turned and hand carved. Decanter and goblets are rosewood and harewood. Salad plates 5½-inch diameter of fiddleback maple. Dinner plates 11-inch diameter of African angico. Utensils are ebony. Teacup and saucer of Brazilian rosewood. Candle holders of African shedua. Fruit bowl of padouk.

JEWELRY CHEST. By Jere Osgood. Bird's-eye maple. Suede-lined drawers. Carved and constructed. 26″ high, 12″ wide, 12″ deep.

*Courtesy, artist*

Covered containers by William Jaquith Evans. Intricately laminated boxes made by machine and hand-carving and construction methods.

BRIERROOT HAND-CARVED PIPE. By Joel Rich. Pipes must be carefully sized and well balanced.

*Courtesy, artist*

Carved pull toy by Jack Farris. A variety of colorful woods carved, assembled, and inlaid.

Photo, Victor Joe Zell

Laminated vase by Charles M. Kaplan. Walnut 10″ high.

Courtesy, artist

By Milon Hutchinson. Pegged bowls and jar holders using a variety of woods.

BEAST. By Norm Tornheim. A crematorial urn of carved walnut with carved bone "spine." 8″ high, 13″ wide, 5″ deep.

By Rita Blum. Laminated and carved wood box with two-part swivel enamel-on-copper top. Approx. 5″ high, 10″ diameter.

Dulcimers by Capri Taurus. Two custom handmade instruments of rosewood, ebony, and spruce.

*Courtesy, Stephen Jackel*

THE HAPPY HOOKER ALARM CLOCK. By Jeffrey Dean. Animated object has little men ringing bells on the bosom when alarm goes off. Knob at base opens doors beneath belly from which a little guy pops out smiling.

*Courtesy, artist*

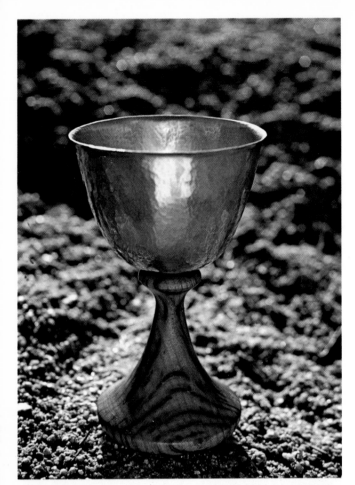

Punch cup by Lawrence B. Hunter. Wood base lathe turned. Cup is brass spun on the lathe.

FEATHER VASE. By Mel Mordaunt. East India rosewood, with laminated birch and walnut inse 6¼″ high. Lathe turned.

*Courtesy, arti*

Vases by Doug Ayers. Hand carved. Yew, osag orange, and apricot woods. 7″ to 9″ high, a about 5″ wide.

Carved wild cherry fruit bowl by Mark Lindquist. 20″ long, 10″ wide.
*Photo, Robert Steinberg, Cambridge, Mass.*

Nutshell bowl by Jon Brooks. Elm wood. 24″ diameter. Carved and hinged.
*Courtesy, artist*

Rosewood bowl by Robert Trout. 2″ high, 7″ wide, 5″ deep. Hand carved.
*Courtesy, artist*

JEWELRY CHEST. By Espenet. A band-saw box of holly with ebony knobs; so called because cuts are made with a band saw. 20″ high, 4″ wide, 5″ deep.

*Courtesy, artist*

Band-saw box by Espenet. Guatemalan gavalea wood. 16″ high, 4″ wide, 4″ deep.

*Courtesy, artist*

Reliquary by Lawrence B. Hunter. Cherry wood with formed leather inset lined with fur. Turquoise figure. 11″ high, 6″ wide, 4″ deep.

Burl bowl by Jack Inhofe. Only a portion of the natural form was carved and finished. *Collection, Lawrence B. Hunter*

Carved salad bowl of bay laurel burl with madrone salad paddle. By Bruce Mitchell. Roughed out with a chain saw and finished with various power and hand tools.
*Courtesy, artist*

Bowl by Jocko Johnson. Walnut, 2″ high, 24″ long, 7″ wide. Insets of lighter wood for the large circle. Gemstones are set in small knotholes. Carved with chain saw and power tools.

Jewelry box by Dennis Lingo of black walnut and rosewood with a rolling top.
*Courtesy, artist*

"McCallister box" by Michael Graham. Angico wood. 7" high, 9" wide, 4" deep.
*Courtesy, artist*

Birdbox by Elizabeth A. Tuttle. Cherry, carved and constructed. 2¼" deep, 9" wide, 12" high.
*Courtesy, artist*

153

*Right:* By John Bickel. Walnut jewel cabinet with turned ebony pulls. 6'' high, 9'' wide, 6 1/2'' deep. The form was first made as a rectangular box and then shaped into smooth flowing curves, using gouges and mallet.

*Courtesy, artist*

*Center:* By John Bickel. Mahogany jewel cabinet with rosewood turned pulls. 6'' high, 19'' wide, 8 1/2'' deep.

*Courtesy, artist*

*Below left and right:* Walnut jewel box (*closed and open views*). By Stephen Robin. 3'' high, 12 1/2'' wide, 9'' deep.

*Photographed at the
Galeria del Sol,
Santa Barbara, California*

*Above:* Bar (*open and closed views*). By Dan L. Valenza. Walnut. 20'' high.

*Photos, artist*

*Right:* Jewel box by LeRoy Hogue. Black walnut. 8 1/2'' high, 14 1/2'' wide, 12'' deep.

*Courtesy, artist*

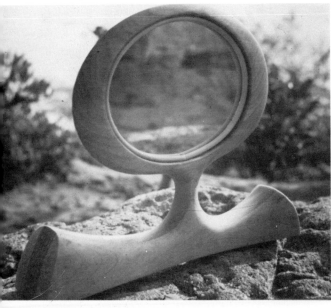

*Above:* Hanging mirror. By Jim Traynor. Rosewood. Approximately 26″ high, 18″ wide.

*Below:* Standing mirror. By Bob Daniells. Birch. 10″ high, 12″ wide, 2 1/4″ deep.

*Above:* Standing mirror. By Stephen R. Johnson. Padouk. 20" high, 14" wide.

*Right*: Standing mirror. By Terry Allen Smith. East Indian rosewood. 6' high.

*Photo, Tom Tramel*

*Opposite above left:* Hand mirror by Frank E. Cummings III. Lignum vitae with dentalium shells and ermine fur at top and ivory band at top of handle. 16" high, 8" wide.

*Opposite above center and right:* By Frank E. Cummings III. Hand mirror (*front and back views*). African blackwood with ivory and dentalium shells. The ivory has been inlaid into the negative "defect" in the wood to make it a positive decorative detail. 16" high, 8" wide.

*Opposite below:* By Frank E. Cummings III. Hand mirror, comb and brush set. Brazilian rosewood, gold and silver peg inlays, javelina bristles.

*Above:* Hand mirror. By Tom Lacagnina. Cherry wood. 3′ high, 20″ long, 12″ wide.

*Courtesy, artist*

*Left: Top to bottom*
By Chris Sabin. Hand mirror. Black walnut frame with African blackwood inset and handle. 6 1/2″ diameter, 12″ long.

*Photo, Joseph Baker*

By Vince Tobaro. Hanging mirror of driftwood partially finished with carving and sanding. 2″ high, 23″ wide, 14″ deep.

*Photographed at the Tarbox Gallery, La Jolla, California*

By William Jaquith Evans. Box mirror. A variety of laminated woods with mirror set on angle for viewing in the bottom of the box. 3″ high, 8″ wide, 4″ deep.

By Sterling King. Four hanging mirrors ranging from 8″ to 11″ in diameter. Two with gouge-chip finish, two smooth. Right mirror has a leather piping trim set in for a raised detail.

*Above and center:* By Elizabeth A. Tuttle. *Birdmirror.* Wings are hinged by leather backing. Cherry wood. 5" high, 8" wide.

*Below:* By Elizabeth A. Tuttle. *Birdbox.* Cherry wood. 2 1/4" high, 12" wide, 9" deep. Mirror with box below. Open view.

*Photos, courtesy artist*

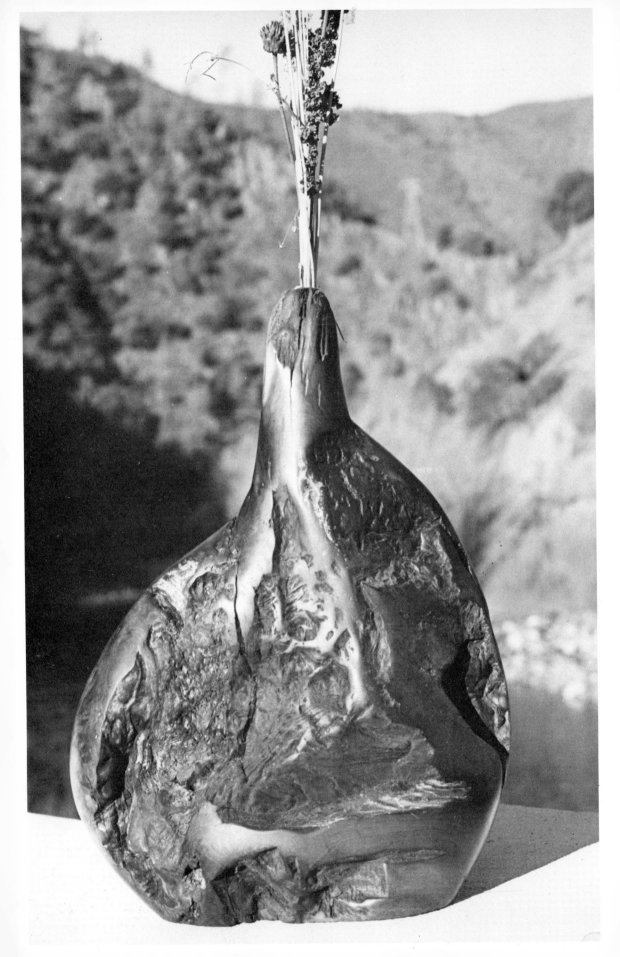

*Opposite:* Manzanita wood weed vase. By Bill Hunter and Harvey Holland. 10″ high, 12″ wide at base, 6″ deep. As below, one side utilizes the natural burl shape while the other is smoothly carved and finished.
*Photographed at Savage's Trading Post, El Portal, California*

Two views of one weed vase. By Bill Hunter and Harvey Holland. Camphorwood. 10″ high, 4″ wide, 5″ deep. The artists utilize the natural wood formation on one side and hand carve the other with a different shaping and fine finish.
*Photographed at Savage's Trading Post, El Portal, California*

Three weed vases of manzanita wood burls by Bill Hunter and Harvey Holland. All combine the natural wood formations with some smoothing and hand finishing. Holes are drilled to accept the weed stems. *Top left:* 9'' high, 7'' wide, 5'' deep. *Below left:* 12'' high, 9'' wide, 5'' deep. *Above:* 9'' high, 7'' wide, 5'' deep.

*Photographed at Savage's Trading Post, El Portal, California*

*Above:* Weed holder by Charles M. Kaplan. Osage orange. Some hand carving with portions of the natural bark for the exterior. 7″ high.

*Courtesy, artist*

*Below:* By Euripides Toro. Approximately 3″ high, 3″ diameter. As much of the original branch or log as possible is retained when the object is shaped and finished.

*Above:* By Euripides Toro. Black walnut double-necked weed vase. 4 1/4″ high, 3″ wide.

*Below:* Geometrically shaped diminutive weed pots of camphorwood. Sizes range from 3 1/2″ to 4 1/2″ high, and 3- to 5-inch bases. *Both, collection Mr. and Mrs. James Goodwin, Hollywood, California*

All photos on these pages are of weed pots by Doug Ayers. Front and back views of the same pots (*above left and center*) illustrate the sculptural quality and different shaping in the two faces of a piece. In all the examples, Doug combines smooth with natural and chiseled surfaces. The varied shapes attest to his personal and sensitive use of the woods that achieve an almost jewellike quality. He uses such woods as apricot, yew, osage orange, shedua, greenheart, lignum vitae, cocobolo, walnut, zebrawood, and others.

*Above:* By Jocko Johnson. Ironwood hookah.

*Top left:* By Harvey Holland and Bill Hunter. Zebrawood pipe and manzanita pipe rack.

*Below:* Harvey Holland and Bill Hunter. Pipe bowls of mixed woods.
*Photographed at
Savage's Trading Post,
El Portal, California*

*Top:* Pipes by Jocko Johnson. Ironwood.

*Center:* By Joel Rich. Intricately
carved brierwood pipes.
                    *Courtesy, artist*

*Below:* By Bill Horgos. Four pipes
combining different kinds of woods.

## CANES AND STAFFS

*Top:* Staff with fantasy carvings of castles. By Jim Pasek. In addition to their function as a walking aid, the staff's castle tops are removable and hold a small vial for medical aids or paraphernalia. Staffs are 64″ long with curved tops of exotic woods such as bubinga, cedar, purpleheart combined with oak and rosewoods. The shafts are usually a hardwood such as oak or ebony for strength.

*Below left:* A screw-off top reveals a place for a small glass vial within. By Jim Pasek.

*Below right:* Walking cane by Jim Pasek has a bird head of cherry wood with rosewood, maple, oak bands and pegs, and an oak and ebony shaft. Carved head is 3″ high, 5″ wide, 1 3/4″ deep.

*Opposite:* A collection of canes antique and modern. *Left to right:* Spanish cane with figures of Christ. English guild figure. Alligators carved on head and handle, from Africa. From Spain, an intricately carved Moorish design with a bird on top. An American cane of maple from about 1880. A contemporary example in parambuke wood with ivory pegs from Durban, South Africa. All about 36″ long.

*Collection, Dr. N. H. Gladstone,*
*Beverly Hills, California*

# MINIATURES

During the research for this book, it was interesting to observe that many artists were intrigued with "miniature" wood objects as something that was "fun" to do but not to take seriously. But Bill Horgos and David Carlin's objects and paraphernalia were very serious works of art. The precedent for miniatures might be the beautiful hand-carved netsukes from Japan often made of wood as well as ivory. The approach, says Mr. Horgos, is more akin to whittling as we think of it in the days of early Americana than to wood carving. Whatever it is, the results are incredible in concept, form, and detail.

All objects on these pages are by Bill Horgos.

*Opposite:*

*Above left:* Mr. & Mrs. Fixit with their anvil, stump, hammer, and mallet are completely hand carved. The largest figure, Mr. Fixit, is only 2 1/8'' high.

*Below left:* Mr. Fixit boxwood hinged box. 2 3/4'' wide.

*Right:* Pie crimper 7'' long. An intricate and precious miniature carving.

*This page top:* Pervert whistle (two views). 4 1/2'' high.

*Below left:* Container in shoe form. Cocobolo. 2 3/4'' high, 3 3/4'' wide.

*Right:* Smuggler. A small container with a lid. 2 1/8'' high.

*Above:* Detail of a *netsuke* from Japan of hand-carved hardwood. About 1 3/4'' diameter.

*Collection, Mr. and Mrs. W. Chapman, Solana Beach, California*

*Below:* By Bill Horgos. Closed and open views of a miniature paraphernalia box. Lignum vitae. 1 3/4'' high, 2 5/8'' wide.

*Top:* By David Carlin. "Weed" pot. Walnut. 2″ high, 1″ wide, 1″ deep.
*Photographed at the Galeria del Sol, Santa Barbara, California*

*Center:* By Bill Horgos. Ebony whistles shaped like a train and like a racing car. Train is 4″ long, car is 2 3/4″ long. Each plays multiple notes.

*Right:* By David Carlin. Container. Laminated woods carved and whittled. The top separates from the bottom below the landscape. 3 1/2″ high, 2 1/2″ wide, 1 inch deep.
*Photographed at the Galeria del Sol, Santa Barbara, California*

## MISCELLANEOUS OBJECTS

The range of useful objects illustrated in this chapter is varied. While many fall into specific categories such as trays, weed pots, miniatures, and so forth, others do not. Therefore, the following pages offer a variety of examples that you may or may not have thought of creating. There may be those you have not associated with a "handmade sculptural-functional object." You will find examples of buttons, buckles, hair ornaments, and weavers' tools, puzzles, doors, and door handles. Most unusual and magnificently crafted are the crematorial urns by Norm Tornheim.

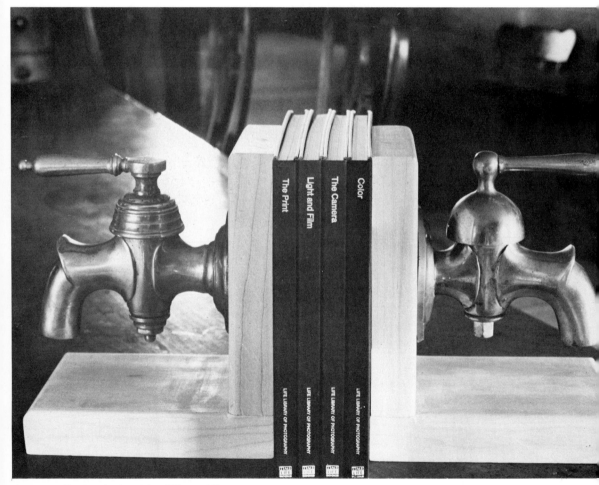

Bookends by John Hilbert. Mixed woods. 12″ high.
*Collection, Mr. and Mrs. Joseph Kraft,*
*Courtesy, Irene Towbin, New York*

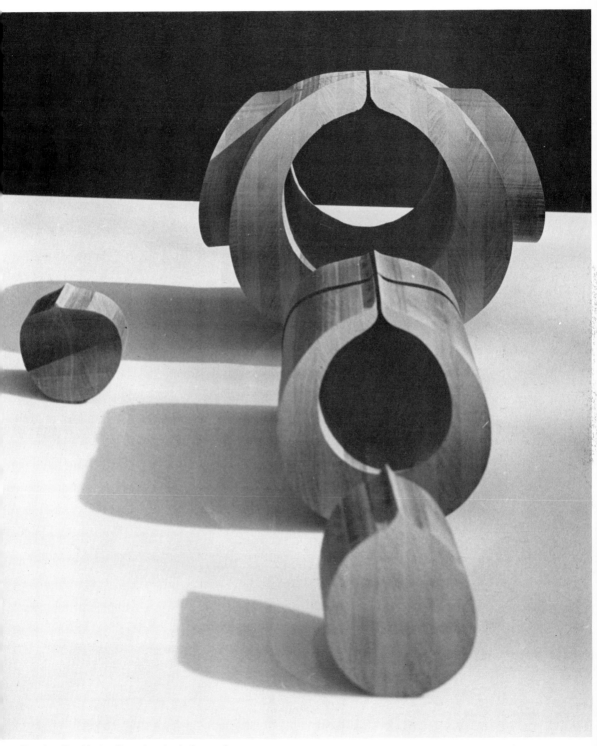

Puzzle. By Marta Pan. Laminated woods.
8″ high.
                    *Courtesy, artist*

Weavers' and crocheters' tools are often handmade. The objects are always held and felt by the hands, and craftspeople working in any medium are receptive to a well-shaped object. *Above and center:* Beaters and crochet hooks in different sizes and of assorted woods.

*Courtesy, "Spin it-Weave it" Studios, El Cajon, California*

*Above right:* By Jay O'Rourke. Pronged hair-sticks of greenheart and goncalo alves woods. They vary in height from 6 to \8 1/4'' and from 3/4-inch to 2-inch width.

*Right:* By Walter Easton. Drop spindles for weaving are birch and cherry wood. 14'' long, 4'' diameter. Lathe turned with hand-carved details.

*Courtesy, artist*

*Right:* By John R. Allan. Netting needle of hand-carved hardwood.

*Below:* Magnifying glass by Lawrence B. Hunter. Walnut. 6″ high, 4″ wide.

*Below right:* A collection of hardwood hand-carved buttons. By Rainbow. 5/8-inch to 1 1/2″ diameter.

*Above left:* By Bill Hanner. Hardwood hand-carved buckles with silver inlays to hold hardware on opposite side.
*Photographed at Savage's Trading Post, El Portal, California*

*Above right:* By John R. Allan. Hardwood buckles.

*Center left:* Hair ornaments by William Jaquith Evans.

*Center right:* By Jocko Johnson. Buckles.
*Collection, Mable Hutchinson, Capistrano Beach, California*

*Below right:* Bracelets by William Jaquith Evans. Teak and walnut.

*Top:* By Lawrence B. Hunter. Animal-shaped speakers. Laminated Finland birch plywood. Each is 10″ high, 8 1/2″ wide, 11″ deep. Chip-carved surface.

*Center:* By Dick Catlett. Cribbage board. "Mother and Kit Beaver" Alder. 20″ long.

*Courtesy, artist*

*Below:* Gavel by Stephen Hogbin. Maple. 7″ long.

*Left:* By Stephen Hogbin. Dustpan handle. Laminated and carved oak, maple, and basswood handle attached to a fender from a Karmann Ghia. 26″ long.

Sculptural shelf unit. By Terry Allen
Smith. Padouk, bubinga, and rose-
wood. 48″ high.
*Courtesy, artist*


Door. By Federico Armijo. Hand-
carved walnut. 7 feet high.
*Courtesy, artist*

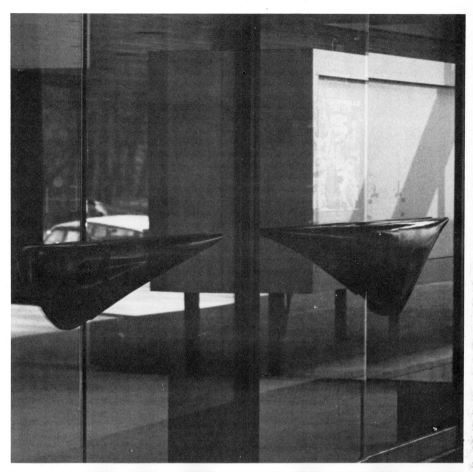

Door handles. By Marta Pan. Stained
wood. 50 pieces installed at the Traditional Crafts Museum, Paris.
                    *Courtesy, artist*

Door handle details by Ed Almquist.
                    *Courtesy, artist*

Norm Tornheim has created unusual sculptural-functional objects to serve as "crematorial urns" for storing ashes. They all have removable stoppers or lids. Each is magnificently handcrafted and some combine woodworking with jewelry techniques and materials.

*Right:* SILVER GHOST. By Norm Tornheim is laminated padouk with rosewood wheels, copper with silver inlay and brass pegs. 6″ high, 19″ wide, 5 1/2″ deep.

*Below:* MOON CHARIOT. By Norm Tornheim. Walnut with silver tubing inlay, Plexiglas cover. Beneath are carved wood bones. 4″ high, 13″ wide, 5 1/2″ deep.

*Below right:* BEAST. By Norm Tornheim. Walnut with bone vertebrae. 8″ high, 13″ wide, 5″ deep.

184

# 6 Inlay and Marquetry

By Tom Taylor. Belt buckle inlaid with a silver circle and radiating smaller circles of silver and gold wire. 3/4-inch high, 2 1/2'' wide, 2'' deep.

*Opposite:* By Enrico Baj. Mixed woods inlaid on a tabletop.

*Courtesy, Galleria Schwarz, Milan, Italy*

By Keith E. Stephens. Two hand-carved bowls with ivory inlay at the tips of the handles. The larger one is rosewood, 7'' high, 14'' wide, 5'' deep. The smaller one is olla wood, 7'' high, 11'' wide, 6'' deep.

The practice of inlaying one or more pieces of wood or other materials into a base piece of wood has been practiced by man since the earliest days and was known in the ancient Egyptian, Babylonian, and Greek civilizations. In *true inlay*, also referred to as *intarsia*, a pattern is cut with chisels in the surface of a wood panel to a depth of about 1/8 to 1/4 inch. The depressions thus produced are then filled with pieces of wood, ivory, shell, horn, metals, or other materials.

*Marquetry* is the process of forming inlaid patterns by inserting pieces of wood, shell, or ivory into a *wood* veneer that is then applied to a wooden object.

Both *true inlay* and *marquetry* are still practiced by woodworkers and continue to be a challenging approach to the embellishment of decorative objects and furniture.

Although both techniques have traditionalism attached to them, it is in the nature of contemporary craftsmen to bend the techniques and the results to their own interpretations. They are offered here to stimulate ideas for applying a variety of inlay in small wood objects where you may not have thought of it before. The craftsman today becomes versed in so many techniques that exposure to silversmithing and jewelry casting, for example, might encourage the inlay of semiprecious metals as in the examples by Keith Stephens. Ann Malmlund improvised an inlay initially to camouflage an imperfection in the wood, but the final result is a unique decorative detail (page 135). The containers by Frank E. Cummings III (page 5) should be studied for application of a variety of inlaid materials including fibers, mirrors, silver, and dentalium. Jocko Johnson's bowls (page 129) often have gemstones placed in a resin bed within a natural or purposely made depression in the wood.

The true inlay, or intarsia, practiced by ancient and medieval woodworkers was always done with hand driven gouges. The same procedures can be accomplished more quickly today by using power routers and other electric hand tools.

Marquetry, however, is done with hand tools. Among the beauties of marquetry is that the easy-to-cut veneers can be handled by anyone of any age, using materials you probably have plus an X-acto knife or a jeweler's saw. It doesn't require an elaborate, spacious work area; it can be done on a kitchen table.

Marquetry is considered either *pictorial* or *applied*. "Pictorial" is the creation of pictures or scenes and "applied" is the making of designs which are used to decorate objects. Bill Brewerton of Rochester, New York, shares his expertise at marquetry in the demonstrations on pages 189 to 195.

The look of inlay can be achieved by other methods as illustrated in the pegging demonstration by William Jaquith Evans. Or it can be accomplished by combining any of the techniques with each other, or using them all together. There is no one way, no right or wrong way, to approach any of the crafts today. If you know what you want to achieve, use any technique to reach the result.

*Opposite above:* By Enrico Baj. Mixed woods inlaid on a tabletop.
*Courtesy, Galleria Schwarz, Milan, Italy*

*Opposite below:* Mid-nineteenth-century English sewing box is made of wood with papier-mâché and inlaid with mother-of-pearl, ivory, silk, and paper, then gilded and painted in parts.
*Courtesy, Cooper-Hewitt Museum of Decorative Arts and Design, Smithsonian Institution, New York*

## MARQUETRY

William E. Brewerton of Rochester, New York, has won innumerable prizes for his marquetry. He demonstrates two approaches to the technique 1) cutting the veneers with an X-acto knife and 2) cutting with a jeweler's saw. The knife method shown in the first series of photos utilizes a pattern with straight lines which makes cutting easy, especially for a first attempt. The complete series of steps for marquetry is shown; the same inlays and finishing procedures are used when the veneers are cut with a saw (page 193).

NORTH GATE OF YORK CATHEDRAL. By
William E. Brewerton. Pictorial marquetry.
*Photo, Sally K. Davidson*

You will need: an X-acto knife with a #11 blade, a ruler, T-square, razor blade, cutting board, masking tape, sanding block with medium and fine sandpapers, rubber cement, wood glue and C-clamps (not shown) or heavy rubber bands for holding the veneer to the object. Assorted veneers of contrasting colors.

You will also need the object to be decorated such as a box, shown here, and a drawing of the pattern you plan to use. The stages of the process are shown: the undecorated box; the walnut background, koa for the dark portions of the star and avodire for the light portions; the shape cut out of one sheet of walnut; and a finished example of inlays. The final step is gluing the inlay to the box.

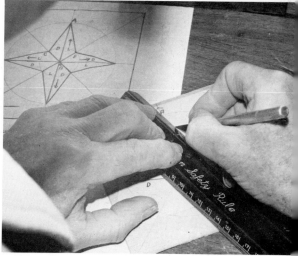

Cut the veneer background approximately 1/8-inch bigger than the box top and cover this with masking tape to make it easier to draw on and cut into. You can trace the design onto the masking tape or draw it on directly.

Place a nonslip ruler (or put tape on the back of any ruler to make it nonslip) and lightly draw the knife along the ruler edge cutting through the tape. This provides a track to guide the knife. Draw the knife along the ruler two or three more times or until the knife point breaks through the other side of the veneer. Do this on all sides to be cut until the star can be removed from the background.

The star is now cut out from the background (*left*). Tape is being placed over the contrasting veneers so it can be cut. Trace the pattern on the tape of the veneer as you did on the star itself.

Tape the contrasting koa veneer over the background wood using the star-shaped hole as your template. The veneer is cut at the edge, not the center. The grain of the veneer should be placed so it runs from the center out to the point of the star.

The parts of the star are cut out. Edges to be joined should be lightly sanded as should the edges of the hole.

The different-colored woods are assembled in the background veneer. When you are sure they fit closely, lightly smear white glue on the edge of the piece and place in the hole of background veneer securing it in place with a small piece of masking tape. Do this on all the points of the star.

The finished inlaid veneer (*left*) is ready to be glued to the box top. Spread glue on the box cover.

Then spread glue on the inlay.

Place the inlay upside down on the box (notice that the tapes are still in place).

Adhere to box top with clamps. Use two pieces of scrap wood larger than the top and sandwich the box top between them to prevent clamps from marking up box and veneer. Let dry thoroughly.

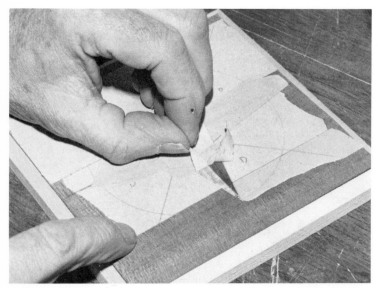

The tape is peeled gently from the box. If the veneer overlaps the edge, trim it down carefully all around.

The entire box should be sanded, using first medium and then fine sandpapers. Electric sanding tools may be used also, very carefully, so as not to disturb the inlay.

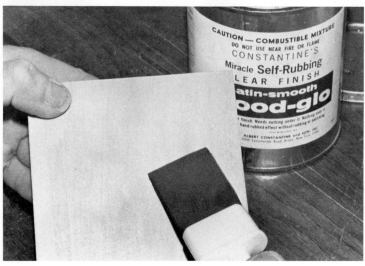

The box is varnished and finished by rubbing with steel wool. It may be waxed, if desired.

*Demonstrations by*
*William E. Brewerton,*
*Photos by Sally K. Davidson*

## THE SAW METHOD

Using a fine jeweler's saw, or a special blade for marquetry on a jigsaw, several layers of veneer can be cut simultaneously. This has the effect of "production" but still retains the handmade quality because the use of different color veneers yields an infinite range of color-in-design possibilities. Although the basic design remains the same, no two veneers need be exactly alike because of the interchange of coloring. Too thick a saw will result in too much kerf, or gap, between the inlay and the background shape. Use a blade as small as a #8 in a jeweler's saw.

When using a saw, the pieces must be taped as with the knife. If more than one veneer is to be cut simultaneously (up to 10 is about the limit), fasten the veneers to one another by coating each piece (except the top) with rubber cement on the tapes (not on the woods). Place pieces of tape around the edges of the layers to keep them secure and place them under a weight until the rubber cement is dry.

To start the holes in the background veneer use a very thin electric drill bit or a needle slightly larger than the saw blade. Make a tiny hole at a corner of each portion of the pattern. The saw blade is pushed through this starting hole and cutting proceeds.

A V-shaped wooden slotted board clamped to a table makes an efficient surface for holding the veneer and allowing the saw to wiggle around the holes. After the pieces are cut, push them out with a pointed object.

Keep the veneer cutouts of each shape in a different container to make it easier to find them when you are ready to inlay. It's a good idea to number above each hole in the background and place each inlay of the corresponding shape in a container with that number.

When multiple pieces of veneers are cut, often the fit of the inlay into the hole is not as accurate as when only one sheet is cut with a knife. If spaces exist between the inlay and the background, these can be filled in with sanded particles of the wood mixed with white glue to make a wood putty consistency.

When you separate the sandwiched veneers that have been held with rubber cement and tape, remove any sticky residue by peeling it off or rubbing lightly with a rag moistened with turpentine. The tape that holds the inlay is removed only *after* the veneer is assembled on the object. Assembling and finishing are accomplished in the same way as in the preceding series on marquetry.

*All demonstrations by William E. Brewerton,*
*Photos, Sally K. Davidson*

A jeweler's saw, or a fretsaw, is used with the teeth of the blade downward toward the handle. One end of the blade is placed in the saw jaw; the blade is then pushed through the tiny hole made in the veneer and the other end tightened into the other jaw of the saw. The blade must be taut.

The saw blade is manipulated around the lines of the pattern. The pieces are then pushed out with a pointed tool.

Inlays cut from one color veneer are placed in the background veneer of a contrasting color. Edges are glued in and any kerf, or gaps, are filled in with sawdust mixed with glue.

*Above:* Small hutch by William E. Brewerton. Marquetry.

*Below:* Music box by William E. Brewerton. Marquetry.

*Photos, Sally K. Davidson*

Traditional marquetry is time consuming and a labor of love. Even if one attempts to reproduce the same design several times, each piece is still individually handcrafted. William Jaquith Evans, himself well versed in marquetry techniques, wanted the beauty of inlaid veneer woods combined with a process that would make the production of the items economical enough to market at craft shows. He insets dowels into blocks of wood using the same principles that Milon Hutchinson demonstrated in his decorative pegged bowls (chapter 3). Will, however, inserts long pegs or dowels into the block and then slices the block into thin veneers or thicker slices depending upon the object to be made. For the earrings, below, he combines a unique approach to laminating with doweling for intricate inlay effects. The mirrors and cigarette holders (page 199) were made of thicker slices of the woods. He demonstrates the doweling technique.

*Left:* First a block of ash and mahogany is laminated. A 5/8-inch-diameter plug is cut with the laminate line across the center to yield a two color plug.

*Below:* Several plugs are cut out of the block and the laminate line may appear randomly across any portion of the surface.

*Above:* A 3/8-inch hole is made in the block of walnut to receive the plug.

*Right center and below:* The plug is glued. Glue is applied with a thinner dowel and the plug placed in the walnut. If the plug needs coaxing to force it into the hole, place another length of dowel in the drill chuck and use the pressure of the machine to push the plug into the walnut. Dry thoroughly.

*Opposite:* By William Jaquith Evans. Earrings, plain and inlaid.

When the first plug is dry, a second hole, 1/2
inch in diameter is drilled. A 1/2-inch plug of
ash has been cut and placed in the second
hole and a third, 3/8-inch hole is drilled and
filled with a walnut plug cut from a grain pattern that differs from the block.

When all plugs are dried in the board (here
two sets have been inlaid), the board is
placed on the band saw and sliced in half
and then in half again and again until a multiple number of thin slices is created. The
slices are reclamped together and the ear-
ring shapes are cut out.

*Above:* Vanity mirrors by William Jaquith Evans. Brazilian rosewood and fiddleback mahogany. Floral patterns are made with a series of overlapped plugs and with veneers laminated in the wood block for stems. Inlay appears on fronts and backs of mirrors.

*Below:* By William Jaquith Evans. Cigarette or playing card boxes. 4″ high, 3 1/2″ wide. Inlaid panels used for fronts and backs with sides added and ends rounded.

*Above:* By Keith E. Stephens. Rosewood bowl with ivory inlay at tip of handle. 14" wide, 3" deep.

*Above left:* By John Bauer. A wall cabinet of madrone and cypress with a hand-sculptured door and inlay. The background oval is teak, the moon is bone, the coat is rosewood, the chicken, feet, and moustache are ebony, and the hat and shirt are boxwood. Other details are purpleheart and amaranth. 23 1/2" high, 19" wide, 6" deep.

*Below:* By John Bauer. Wall hanging knife holders inlaid with teak, rosewood, madrone, and other woods. The left holder has a cherry front and acacia back. The right one is walnut and acacia.

*Above and below:* By Keith E. Stephens. Rosewood box with silver inlay. 2″ high, 3″ wide, 7″ long. Silver pulls at the ends lock the cover in place. Detail of cover.

*Above:* Mirror by Robert Salleroli. Dowels inlaid in a frame are used so that the length of the dowels form a pattern and slanted line; the round end cuts form a counterpoint and appear in three different diameters. 51 1/2″ high, 32″ wide.

*Courtesy, artist*

*Below:* By Al Miele. Marquetry. Jewelry box with secret compartment. 3″ high, 12″ wide, 8″ deep. English walnut box with inlay of ebony, tulip-wood, and brass.

*Courtesy, artist*

Ideas for wood inlays for relief patterning.
*Photographed at California
State University, Northridge*

*Opposite:* By Christopher Sabin. Cutting
board. Curly swamp maple with African
blackwood inlay. 18″ high, 8″ wide.
*Photo, Fred Weiss*

Letter stand by Conway Pierson. Birch, hickory,
walnut, and bronze castings with a ceramic pot.
24″ high, 20″ wide, 20″ deep. Hand-carved
wood parts are assembled using refinished wheels
from fishnet hoops. The stand arm is a snath, the
handle of a scythe.

*Courtesy, artist*

# 7 Constructing and Carving

*Above:* Magazine rack by Conway Pierson. 24''
high, 24'' wide, 10'' deep. Cherry, walnut, ash,
birch, with tiny bronze animals and a ceramic pot.
The legs are made from ax handles.

*Right:* Fern stand by Conway Pierson. Laminated
walnut and ash, spruce, with white chicken
feathers, bronze, and a ceramic pot.

*Photos, courtesy, artist*

Joinery, the practice of uniting or combining pieces of wood to extend the dimension in length, thickness, or width, or to change direction, has been used by woodworkers for countless years. Until the use of glue, only joinery was used for butting together edges of wood, mitering corners, pegging, and so forth.

Small objects do not receive the stress and wear qualities of heavier wood items such as furniture, floors, and ships, but the application of basic joints to create boxes, jewelry cabinets, musical instruments, toys, and other useful accessories is an important part of the craftsman's working vocabulary. A joint is often a visual as well as functional detail. For example, a box corner could be made by butting two pieces of wood but a dovetail joint will add measurably to the visual quality of the box. The joint may be made from a different wood so it will contrast with the color of the basic structural wood.

There are about a dozen much-used woodworking joints, and each has several variations. An assortment of joints used in small objects is pictured on the following pages. These can be made by observing the drawings and cutting the parts to shape with saw and chisels. Directions for creating compound and more complex joints can be found in handyman's magazines and in carpentry and woodworking books listed in the bibliography.

Practically all joints may be reinforced with glues and/or fasteners such as nails, screws, pins, wedges, splints, dowels, corrugated fasteners, and other hardware, depending upon the stress that will be put on the joint.

The stress that a joint will receive will usually determine how it will be made. The contents of a drawer resist the effort you apply when you pull the drawer out. All the strain is on the joint connecting the drawer front to the sides and, therefore, dovetails are usually used. The interlocking feature resists the strain and will continue to do so even if the glue dries out. A pegged joint will do the same job and is easier to make than the dovetail.

The strength of any joint depends largely on the accuracy of the fit to the joining members, the quality of the glue, and the efficiency with which the pieces have been glued and clamped. Other factors that affect the strength of the joint are the porosity of the woods being joined, how the glue adheres to the fibers, and the degree of movement in the wood, that is: how much it swells and contracts under varying humidity conditions. The standard of workmanship is, of course, of utmost importance.

Intricate joints are time consuming and, if an object is made for a selling market, it is more economical timewise to use the simpler joints. You may want to make the intricate joints for the sake of craftsmanship and to enhance the appeal of the object. All the factors must be weighed when you design and create the object.

In addition to usual joinery methods, many of the following examples employ inventive solutions for connecting parts such as handmade hinges, movable joints, hand-turned wood screws, and others. Often the joinery and construction have been so perfectly concealed that the object appears to have been hand carved from a solid piece of wood. In a few examples, such as musical instruments, the objects are not constructed, only carved and these have been placed here for the sake of organization rather than method. The two procedures, constructing and carving, are so compatible that placement of some items in one chapter rather than another was an arbitrary selection.

Jewelry cabinet (*two views*) by Elisabeth Krisel. Constructed parts made of laminated molded plywood. English brown oak veneer and burl, brass pieces turned on a machine lathe. 12″ high, 9″ diameter.

*Courtesy, artist*

SIMPLE JOINTS

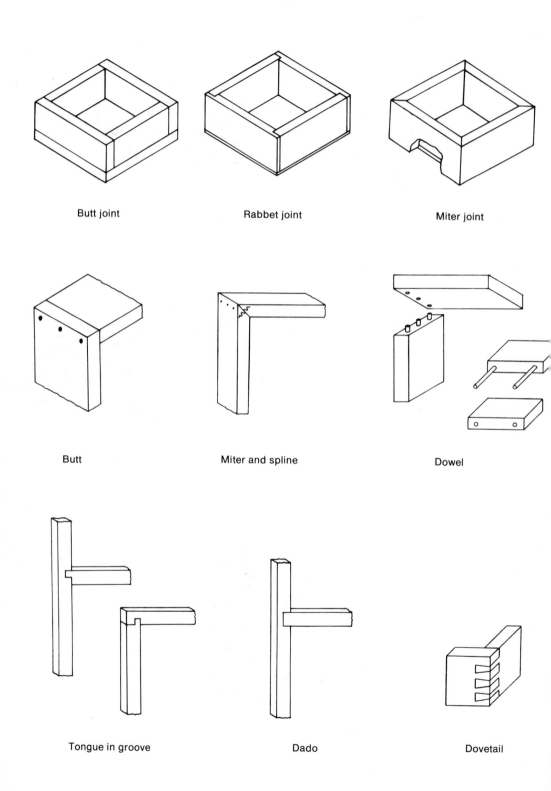

Butt joint          Rabbet joint          Miter joint

Butt          Miter and spline          Dowel

Tongue in groove          Dado          Dovetail

APPLICATION OF JOINTS IN DIFFERENT COLORED WOODS          *Examples by Lawrence B. Hunter*

Half lapped and cross lapped

Dado

Dovetail

Wedge peggings

Box joint

Blocks of wood, intricately carved with geometric patterns, can be used any way the imagination dictates. The squares can be used for box tops, assembled for tables, doors, and applied on other objects. Milon Hutchinson shares his methods for carving the blocks using the radial arm saw with the indexing concept already shown in chapter 3. He places the block on the indexer and makes cuts in many directions. "You have to play around with it," says Milon, "until you get the feel of what the saw will do at different progressive settings." Linear designs can be combined with circular forms made on the drill press with circle cutters or with router cuts.

*Left:* The block has a hole in the back that fits on a peg to hold it tightly to the indexing wheel. A stopboard is also on the holding surface.

*Below:* The first cut is made.

The index is turned one preset notch for each cut and for as many cuts as desired on one side of the block. The lever fits into pre-bored holes in a circle. By changing the number of holes between cuts, different designs result.

When the block is turned and cut from the other side, the geometric design in the center becomes apparent.

Edges are safely and easily beveled on a Rockwell uniplane which can make micro-meterlike cuts any angle from 0° to 45°.

Shredded sandpaper in a Sand-o-Flex grinding wheel makes quick work of smoothing the grooves.

A small assortment of the myriad possibilities of carving in this manner.
*Demonstration by Milon Hutchinson*
*Photos, author*

Spinning wheel by Bob Daniells. Hand carved and constructed. Red oak and walnut. 36'' high, 36'' wide, 14'' deep.

*Detail at right:* All parts can be dismantled. Metal spokes are held to the wheels by pegs; all gears, nuts, axles, and wood parts are hand carved and lathe turned.

*Above:* Hand-carved clock mechanism by John Gaughan (*detail of large grandfather clock*). Brazilian rosewood. The wood gears perform functionally but their interacting parts create a kinetic sculptural motion.

*Right:* CLOCK III (*detail*). A handcrafted clock by Lawrence B. Hunter. Laminated and carved cherry wood. The concept of the hand-carved escapement suggests a fanciful animal whose head moves slowly, perpetually, back and forth.

*Top:* By Tom Bendon. Pau ferro clock case. 8″ high. Electronics by Ed Muns.
*Courtesy, Tom Bendon*

*Below:* Two clocks by Jere Osgood for wall or desk use. Battery powered. The larger one is made of goncalo alves with a maple face. 11″ high, 9 1/2″ wide, 2 3/4″ deep. The smaller clock has a cherry wood case with a figured maple and walnut face.
*Courtesy, artist*

*Top:* By Tom Bendon. Pau ferro clock case. 8″ high. Electronics by Ed Muns.
*Courtesy, Tom Bendon*

*Below:* By John Gaughan. Brazilian rosewood with two chrome balls that operate on a magnetic field principle. 2 1/4″ high, 8 1/4″ square.

*Top:* Fantasy radio cabinet of laminated woods by Wilfred Malmlund. 34" high, 18" wide, 12" deep.

*Below:* Clock radio by John Bickel. American black walnut with rosewood knobs. 4 1/2" high, 12 1/2" wide, 4 1/2" deep. The cabinet was constructed as a rectangular box, then shaped with a band saw, gouges, and mallet.

*Courtesy, artist*

Telephone by Richard Frinier. Four views. Teak and East Indian rosewood, padouk handles, mirror, and raised copper parts. Closed, the piece appears as a sculptural form with a mirror. Open, and with the receiver removed, it becomes a functioning telephone that may be wired and the mechanism assembled into the wood housing. Top right shows the receiver removed and the base which holds the mouthpiece pulled forward. Below right illustrates the arrangement of wood parts to allow back and forth movement. The platform also serves as a writing shelf.

Another telephone cabinet by Richard Frinier. Closed and open views. East Indian and Brazilian rosewood with formed leather center at the mouthpiece area. Horsehair hangs at bottom of removable part that becomes the receiver. 24″ high, 8 1/2″ wide, 4″ deep.

*Opposite:* Covered container by Lawrence R. Jones. Three views. Nara wood body with Brazilian rosewood legs. Some lathe-turned parts with hand-carved details and legs. 13'' high, 6'' wide.

*Courtesy, artist*

Covered container by Lawrence R. Jones. Brazilian rosewood, with bronze cover. 13'' high, 6'' wide.

By Robert Strini. A jewelry box with drawers and adjustable mirror on a swinging bar. 5 1/2' high. A variety of laminated woods with a bird's-eye maple heart-shaped drawer. Open and closed views and details.

*Photos, artist*

By Bob Daniells. Jewelry chest of red oak and
walnut. 27'' high, 7'' wide, 7'' deep.
Drawers pull out (*right*). Because the narrower
dimension at the top makes the drawers difficult
to get into, they are hinged to open sideways.

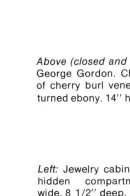

*Above (closed and open views):* Jewelry box by George Gordon. Cherry with the drawer fronts of cherry burl veneer. The drawer handles are turned ebony. 14" high, 25" wide, 10 1/2" deep.
*Collection, Mrs. Jody Todd*
*Rochester, New York*
*Photos, artist*

*Left:* Jewelry cabinet by Hal Ross. Teak with a hidden compartment. 17 1/4" high, 8" wide, 8 1/2" deep.

*Photo, artist*

*Above:* By Wayne Raab. Black walnut box dovetailed and carved. 5'' high, 10'' wide, 4'' deep.

*Courtesy, artist*

*Above left:* ANNIVERSARY PIECE by Lyle Laske. Of teak and ebony with a Sarna bell within. 10 1/2'' high, 15'' wide, 6'' deep.

*Collection, Francine Laske*
*Courtesy, artist*

*Center left:* By Lyle Laske. Wedding chest. Teak. 14'' high, 20'' wide, 8'' deep.
*Collection, Mr. and Mrs. Sol Koppel*
*Courtesy, artist*

*Below left:* By William Jaquith Evans. Laminated and constructed jewelry box with pegged inlays. 6 1/2'' high, 8'' wide, 5'' deep.

*Above left:* By Mark Paulson. Jewelry cabinet. Cherry with maple panels. 28″ high, 18″ wide.

*Above right:* By Mark Paulson. Hat rack with mirrors. Cherry. 22″ high, 14″ wide.

*Below (open and closed views):* By Mark Paulson. Collector's box that holds a piece of a shell. Cherry and vermilion. 8″ high, 8″ wide.

*All photos, courtesy artist*

*Above:* By William Jaquith Evans. Distressed red-wood case constructed and carved to hold the handmade raised sterling silver wine goblets. Felt lining is added where cups are placed. 11″ high, 20 1/2″ wide, 3 1/2″ deep.

*Below left:* By William Jaquith Evans. Ring display cabinet. Walnut. Dovetailed and assembled with four removable panels for displaying the rings horizontally. Each ring fits into a slot that has a hidden sliding bar that holds it in place.

*Below right:* Dulcimer case by Lawrence R. Jones. Brazilian rosewood, walnut, and mahogany. 6″ high, 13″ wide.

*Above:* Pipe holder (*two views*) by Skip Benson. American black walnut. 12″ high, 24″ wide, 14″ deep. Laminated endpieces assembled to flat sidepieces and shaped.

*Courtesy, artist*

*Below:* By William Jaquith Evans. Asparagus steamer (*closed and open views*). Laminated wood and metal. 12″ high, 18 1/2″ wide, 5″ deep. A funky object made as a joke; but it works.

## MUSICAL INSTRUMENTS

The handmade musical instrument is a challenge for the craftsman to create. He must select woods that can be worked easily and will produce the necessary tonal qualities, that are lightweight, yet strong, and have a beauty of grain as well. It is likely that musical instruments actually existed before there were men to use them. Nature's own materials provide the ideas for many instruments. A split reed or piece of loose bark set vibrating or swaying by the wind produces sounds along the same principles as the reed or bark used in making present-day clarinets and oboes.

There are volumes written about the history of musical instruments and their creation. Modern craftsmen utilize elaborate examples and proceed to simplify them or add their own interpretations to the shapes, the ways they are finished, and to the cases that carry them. J. B. Blunk handcarves redwood root for percussion instruments; Trevor Robinson uses a lathe and some hand carving to create sleek, clean clarinets and flutes; Lawrence Jones, Peter McQueen, Harriet Matthews, and Capri Taurus's stringed instruments are one of a kind, lovingly made, constructed and carved pieces.

*Above:* West African thumb piano. Wood with metal. 2″ high, 10″ wide, 4″ deep. Played to keep evil spirits away.

Collection, Mr. and Mrs. W.
Chapman,
Solana Beach, California

Whistle. Brazilian rosewood. Hand carved, with reeds pegged so they hang free within each end to produce sound.

Collection, author

*Above:* By Trevor Robinson. Lathe-turned and hand-finished flutes (*top*) in various woods. Clarinet (*below*) of cherry wood. 17'' long.

*Courtesy, artist*

*Left:* Bolivian flute, carved and painted with added mouthpiece and reed. 12 1/2'' high, 1 1/4'' square.

*Collection, author*

*Right:* By J. B. Blunk. Redwood root. The instruments are played by hitting one side as a drum and by rubbing the stick along the toothed side for a grating sound. Heights: 10'', 11'' and 12''.

*Top and center:* Musical instruments by Peter McQueen. *Left to right, front and back views:* Mandolin, six string guitar, six string guitar, and twelve string guitar. Woods are teak with vermilion inlay, vermilion with maple inlay, walnut with multi-fancy inlay with either maple or mahogany necks. Sizes are from 10" x 26" to 13" and 34".

*Courtesy, Deson-Zaks Gallery,
Chicago, Illinois*

*Below left and right:* By Lawrence R. Jones. Dulcimer with a soundboard of Sitka spruce, fingerboard of Brazilian rosewood with ivory inlay, and sides and back of Brazilian rosewood. Case is made of koa and Brazilian rosewood. 3" high, 38" long, 12" deep.

*Courtesy, artist*

Dulcimer by Capri Taurus. Rosewood, ebony, and spruce.

*Courtesy, Stephen Jackel,*
*Capri Taurus Dulcimers,*
*Felton, California*

*Top and below right:* By Harriett Matthews. Dulcimer of cherry wood using a heat bending technique for the sides. 2 1/4" high, 34" long, 7 1/2" deep. Ebony pegs. Hand-carved figure at end.

*Courtesy, artist*

## TOYS

Handmade toys are surely art, and like any other art form they can be ordinary or beautiful, simple or ornate. Actually, the first toys of prehistory are regarded by the art historian as "sculpture" and not toys at all. In ancient Egypt a high priest would literally climb into a religious object that had moving arms, heads, and mouths, and "play" with the parts just as with a toy. Some authorities even considered dubbing these as early "kinetic" sculptures. Whatever the classification, the creation of toys is the creation of functional sculpture and the examples shown emphasize that premise.

A toy can be carved out of a block of wood and the result can be as simple and abstract, yet recognizable, a shape as those made by sculptor Hugh Townley. They can be as intricately designed with each piece beautifully carved and joined to others as those by Stephen R. Johnson.

Many craftsmen make toys simply because they are *fun.* Then they discover that handmade toys sell despite the colossal toy manufacturing industry. They discover that children gravitate toward the natural wood, hardcrafted object, while parents who buy toys believe the child prefers the gaudy, brightly colored plastic replica of a real object. One craftsman always lets the child for whom he's making a toy select the colors, and invariably they will be quiet, muted tones.

In designing toys, several factors come into play. The theme must be simple so the object is recognizable. It should capture the mood and concept of the real object without locking in the imagination too closely. When designing, you must decide on the proportions, amount of detail, weight, and texture.

It is best to design from the real object rather than from another toy. If you're going to design an airplane, look at real planes to determine the relationship of the wings to the body, the height of the piece, the shape of the front and the tail and roughly determine the basic proportions. If you plan to give it human characteristics such as eyes, month, and so forth, make these humorous and emphasize them.

Sketch the object and then edit out the details, keeping just enough to capture the concept and eliminating extraneous ones. Cut the pattern out of paper if you like and then trace, or sketch it onto the wood and cut out the parts needed. Tack the toy together and make sure it looks right, that all the parts fit. Assemble it, glue, sand, and finish.

There is little in toymaking to limit your imagination. If you are stifled for ideas, ask children what they would like for toys. Have them sketch their own idea. Wayne Kreuger's hedgehog house (page 235) is an example of a sketch made by a child. Mr. Kreuger developed the custom-made toy from the child's drawing and created a house he could never have envisioned himself.

Types of toys, such as puppets, banks, puzzles, push and pull toys, can be culled from the toy shelves but for actual design, the one-of-a-kind toymaker can outcreate the manufactured item for quality of workmanship and the ultimate in a sculptural and functional form of art.

*Opposite and top:* Mouse and turtle by Hugh Townley exhibit minimal carving to capture the gesture of the figure. Mahogany.
*Courtesy, artist*

Other toys by Chuck Wiley are simply carved in stylized shapes with plywood wheels added. Light engraving, woodburning, and painting for details. Car of the future. Coupe and truck 9″ to 12″ long.
*Photos, Fran H. Kumin*

*Top:* By Jack Farris. Bird is made of seven different hardwoods. Willow body, African padouk comb, African satinwood beak, beech wings, rosewood pull knob, and walnut wheels. The snail shell is Hawaiian koa, head is African padouk, walnut wheels, birch and rosewood pull knob. Each is 7″ high and has eccentric rear end action.

*Photos, Victor Joe Zell*

*Center:* By Deborah D. Bump. A four-piece hippo puzzle assembled and apart. Animal-shaped laminated wood banks at right.

*Courtesy, artist*

*Right:* PORKY-PINE by Craig Carey. Hard maple with maple dowel rods. 5″ high, 7″ wide. The toy is also a bank.

*Courtesy, artist*

*Above:* ROCKA FELLA. Rocking peacock by Bob Daniells. Laminated and constructed red oak, Honduras mahogany, birch, and walnut, 48″ high, 38″ wide, 15″ deep. Tail (*detail photo above right*) made by insetting large and small circles.

*Below:* By Hanna Bauer. Painted puzzle. Shapes made on jigsaw and set in frame.

*Right:* HEDGEHOG HOUSE by Wayne O. Krueger. Assembled and carved painted wood designed from a child's drawing. 36″ high, 24″ wide, 18″ deep.

*Photo, Jesse Alexander*

*Above:* By Stephen R. Johnson. Dump truck. Yellow poplar. 6″ high, 16″ long.

*Below:* By Stephen R. Johnson. Train, yellow poplar. 4″ high, 17″ long.

*Opposite top:* THE CIRCUS by Daniel B. and Deborah D. Bump.  Pine, mahogany, and bird's-eye maple.

*Photo, Daniel B. Bump*

*Opposite center and bottom:* By Stephen R. Johnson. Airplane of yellow poplar. 7″ high, 14″ wide. Crane truck of yellow poplar, 11″ high, 16″ long.

# Selected Bibliography

There are many more books available in each category listed below. Consult the library references: *Subject Guide to Books in Print* for current books, and *The Cumulative Book Index* for current books and books that are no longer in print but still available through libraries.

## I. WOOD TECHNOLOGY

Beekman, W. B. *Elsevier's Wood Dictionary*, 3 volumes. Amsterdam, London, New York: Elsevier Publishing Company, 1964.

Berry, James Berthold. *Wood Identification.* New York: Dover Publications, 1966.

Constantine, Albert, Jr. *Know Your Woods.* New York: Charles Scribner's Sons, 1959.

Dechamps, Roger. *How to Understand the Structure of Hardwood.* Belgium: Musée Royal de L'Afrique Centrale. English translation, 1973.

Edlin, Herbert L. *What Wood Is That?* New York: The Viking Press, 1969.

Hackett, Donald F., and Spielman, Patrick E. *Modern Wood Technology.* Glencoe, Illinois: Bruce Publishing Company, 1968.

Harrar, E. S. *Hough's Encyclopaedia of American Woods*, 13 volumes. New York: Robert Speller and Sons, 1957.

Hunt, George M., and Garratt, George A. *Wood Preservation.* New York: McGraw-Hill Book Company, 3rd edition, 1967.

Sloane, Eric. *Reverence for Wood.* New York: Ballantine Books, 1965.

## II. WOODWORKING

Brown, Emmett and Cyril. *Polychromatic Assembly for Wood Turning*, England: published by The Society of Ornamental Turners. n.d.

Campkin, Marie. *Introducing Marquetry.* New York: Drake Publishers, Inc. n.d.

DeCristoforo, R. J. *Complete Book of Power Tools.* New York: Popular Science Publishing Co., Inc., and Harper and Row, 1972.

————. *Fun with a Saw,* New York: McGraw-Hill Book Company, 1961.

————. *Modern Power Tool Woodworking.* Raymond, Mississippi: Magna Publications, 1967.

*Encyclopaedia Britannica.* Chicago: Encyclopaedia Britannica, Inc., 1969.
Listings under:  Carpentry
                 Marquetry
                 Wood
                 Wood carving
                 Woodworking

Fletcher, Michael J. *Making Wooden Toys.* London: B. T. Batsford, Ltd., and New York: Drake Publishers, Inc., 1972.

Forgione, Joseph, and McIlhany, Sterling. *Wood Inlay: Art and Craft.* New York: Van Nostrand Reinhold Company, 1973.

Groneman, Chris H. *General Woodworking.* New York: McGraw-Hill Book Company, 1971.

Haines, Ray E., et al. *The Wood-Turning Lathe.* New York: Van Nostrand Company, Inc., 1952.

Hammond, James J.; Donnelly, Edward T.; Harrod, Walter F.; Rayner, Norman A. *Woodworking Technology.* Bloomington, Illinois: McKnight & McKnight Publishing Company, 1972.

Hayes, Vincent M. *Artistry in Wood.* New York: Drake Publishers, Inc., 1972.

Hayward, Charles H. *Making Toys in Wood.* New York: Drake Publishers, Inc., 1974.

Hooper, John. *Handcraft in Wood.* Philadelphia and New York: J. B. Lippincott Company, 1953.

Klenke, William W. *The Art of Woodturning.* Peoria, Illinois: Chas. A. Bennett Co., Inc., 1954.

Lincoln, William A. *The Art and Practice of Marquetry: An Introduction to a Forgotten Craft.* New York: Charles Scribner's Sons, 1974.

Maglinley, C. J. *Toys You Can Build.* New York: A. S. Barnes & Co., 1973.

Nilsson, A. *Woodware.* New York: Drake Publishers, Inc., 1973.

Schutze, Rolf. *Making Wooden Toys.* New York: Reinhold Publishing Corporation, 1967.

Stevenson, Peter. *The Art of Making Wooden Toys.* Philadelphia: Chilton Book Co., 1971.

Stokes, Gordon. *Modern Wood Turning.* New York: Drake Publishers, Inc., 1973.

Tangerman, E. J. *The Modern Book of Whittling and Woodcarving.* New York: McGraw-Hill Book Company, 1973.

Williams, Christopher. *The Craftsman of Necessity.* New York: Random House, 1974.

Young, David Russell. *The Steel String Guitar: Construction and Repair.* Radnor, Pennsylvania: Chilton Book Co., 1975.

## III. HISTORY, DESIGN, MISCELLANEOUS

Barilli, Renato. *Art Nouveau.* London and New York: Paul Hamlyn, 1966.

Boericke, Art, and Shapiro, Barry. *Handmade Houses.* San Francisco: The Scrimshaw Press, 1973.

Bushell, Raymond. *The Wonderful World of Netsuke.* Rutland, Vermont, and Tokyo: Charles E. Tuttle Co., 1964.

————. California Design IX, X, XI. Pasadena, California: Pasadena Museum, 1965, 1968, 1971.

Carstenson, Cecil C. *The Craft and Creation of Wood Sculpture.* New York: Charles Scribner's Sons, 1971.

Holt, Claire. *Art in Indonesia.* Ithaca, New York: Cornell University Press, n.d.

Horton, Robin. *Kalabari Sculpture.* Federal Republic of Nigeria, Department of Antiquities, 1965.

Leuzinger, Elsy. *The Art of Africa.* New York: Crown Publishers, Inc., 1960.

Luzzato-Bilitz, Oscar. *Oriental Lacquer.* London, New York, Toronto: Paul Hamlyn, 1966.

Meilach, Dona Z. *Contemporary Art with Wood.* New York: Crown Publishers, Inc., 1968.

————. *Creating Modern Furniture—Trends, Techniques, Appreciation.* New York: Crown Publishers, Inc., 1975.

Muensterberger, Warner. *Sculpture of Primitive Man.* New York: Harry N. Abrams, 1955.

————. *New International Encyclopedia of Art.* New York: The Greystone Press, 1967.

Nordness, Lee. *Objects: U.S.A.* New York: Viking Press, 1970.

Pinto, Edward H. *Treen and Other Wooden Bygones.* London: G. Bell & Sons, 1969.

————. *Treen, or Small Woodware Through the Ages.* London: B.T. Batsford, Ltd., 1949.

————, and Eva. *Turnbridge and Scottish Souvenir Woodware.* London: G. Bell & Sons, 1970.

Rich, Jack C. *Sculpture in Wood.* New York: Oxford University Press, 1970.

Trowell, Margaret, and Nevermann, Hans. *African and Oceanic Art.* New York: Harry N. Abrams, Inc., 1968.

Underwood, Leon. *Figures in Wood of West Africa.* London: A. Tirati, 1951.

## IV. GOVERNMENT PUBLICATIONS

Department of Agriculture, Washington, D.C. 20250
    *Identification of Furniture Woods*, The Circular No. 66.
    *Trees*, Yearbook 1949.

Department of Agriculture, Forest Products
    Laboratory, P.O. Box 5130, Madison, Wisconsin 53705
    *Bending Solid Wood to Form.*
    *Blood Albumin Glues.*
    *Casein Glue.*
    *Effect of Nail Points on Resistance to Withdrawal, The.*
    *Important Factors in Gluing with Animal Glue.*
    *Occurrence and Removal of Glue Stains.*
    *Some Methods of Gluing Light Laminated or Plywood Curved Shapes from Veneer.*
    *Strength of Commercial Liquid Glues.*
    *Strong and Weak Glue Joints.*
    *Vegetable Glue.*
    *Wood as an Engineering Material.*
    *Wood Handbook.*

Department of Agriculture, Forest Service, Washington, D.C. 20250
    *Hardwoods of the South.*
    *Useful Trees of the United States:*
        *Birch*, No. 22
        *Cedar*, No. 14
        *Eastern Hemlock*, No. 10
        *Oak*, No. 20
        *Redwood*
        *Sweetgum*, No. 28
        *Western Hemlock*, No. 11

Department of Commerce, Superintendent of Documents
    Government Printing Office, Washington, D.C. 20402
    *American Hardwoods and Their Uses.*
    *American Southern Pine.*

# Wood Associations

The following professional associations have answered a current questionnaire regarding location and literature available. In some cases, the number of brochures offered were too lengthy to list. Write for titles and price lists. All listings subject to change.

| | | |
|---|---|---|
| American Plywood Association<br>1119 A Street<br>Tacoma, Washington 98401 | Construction Literature<br>Catalog of Handy Plans | Charges |
| Appalachian Hardwood<br>    Manufacturers, Inc.<br>Room 408, NCNB Building<br>High Point, North Carolina 27260 | Booklets and<br>Brochures | Free |
| California Redwood Association<br>617 Montgomery Street<br>San Francisco, California 94111 | Ideas and Plans | Some Free;<br>Some Nominal<br>Charge |
| Fine Hardwoods—<br>    American Walnut Association<br>666 Lake Shore Drive<br>Chicago, Illinois 60611 | Variety of Literature<br><br>16mm Sound Film | Charges<br><br>Charges |
| Hardwood Plywood<br>    Manufacturers Association<br>P. O. Box 6246<br>Arlington, Virginia 22206 | Technical Literature<br>Plans<br>List of Suppliers | Nominal<br>Charges |
| National Hardwood Lumber<br>    Association<br>332 South Michigan<br>Chicago, Illinois 60604 | Technical Information | Nominal<br>Charge |
| Southern Hardwood Lumber<br>    Manufacturers Association<br>805 Sterick Building<br>Memphis, Tennessee 38103 | Booklets and Technical<br>Guides | Free or<br>Nominal<br>Charge |
| Western Wood Products<br>    Association<br>1500 Yeon Building<br>Portland, Oregon 97204 | Plans and Ideas<br>Product Manual | Free or<br>Nominal<br>Charge |

# Sources for Supplies

The following supply sources are listed for your convenience. Materials offered and charges for samples and catalogs are subject to change without notice. No endorsement or responsibility is implied by the author. Price lists are free unless specified. Retail mail order unless otherwise noted.

An updated annually revised listing of suppliers of woods and woodworking tools and equipment can be found in the following publications available at your library or from the publishers: *Contemporary Crafts Market Place*, compiled by American Crafts Council. R.R. Bowker, 1180 Avenue of the Americas, New York, New York 10036. *The Mail Order Crafts Catalog* by Margaret A. Boyd. Chilton Book Co., Radnor, Pennsylvania 19089

| | | |
|---|---|---|
| Robert M. Albrecht<br>8635 Yolanda Avenue<br>Northridge, California 91324 | Changing supply of usual domestic, imported, tropical, rare hardwoods, glues, hand & power tools, abrasives, finishes | Catalog—prices for woods quoted on request |
| Dick Blick Company<br>P.O. Box 1267<br>Galesburg, Illinois 61401 | Hand tools | Catalog |
| Boin Arts & Crafts Co.<br>91 Morris Street<br>Morristown, New Jersey 07960 | Wood kits, glues, hand and power tools, abrasives | Catalog $1, deductible from first order |
| Brookstone Company<br>Peterborough, New Hampshire 03458 | Glues, hand and power tools, abrasives, finishes. Orders shipped on day received. One hundred percent guarantee with full refunds on all merchandise | Catalog |
| Craftsman Wood Service<br>2729 South Mary Street<br>Chicago, Illinois 60608 | Domestic, imported & exotic woods, glues, hand and power tools, abrasives, finishes | Catalog 50¢ for postage & handling |
| Crowe & Coulter<br>Box 484 CP<br>Cherokee, North Carolina 28719 | Large solid blocks of cherry, mahogany, poplar, walnut | Brochure |
| Curtis Woodcraft Supply Co.<br>344 Grandview<br>Memphis, Tennessee 38111 | Woods, usual and exotic, glues, Ashley Iles hand tools, abrasives, finishes | Catalog, retail and wholesale |

| | | |
|---|---|---|
| Educational Lumber Co., Inc.<br>P.O. Box 5373<br>Asheville, North Carolina 28803 | Usual and some exotic woods | Catalog |
| Japan Woodworker (The)<br>1806 Bancroft Way<br>Berkeley, California 94703 | High-quality Japanese chisels, wooden planes and other hand tools | Catalog 50¢ |
| Minnesota Woodworkers<br>Supply Company<br>Rogers, Minnesota 55374 | Veneers, glues, hand tools, abrasives, finishes | Catalog 50¢ |
| Frank Mittermeier, Inc.<br>3577 East Tremont Avenue<br>Bronx, New York 10465 | Hand and power tools, abrasives | Brochure, retail and wholesale |
| Sculpture House, Inc.<br>38 East 30th Street<br>New York, New York 10016 | Usual and exotic woods, hand and power tools | Catalog, retail and wholesale |
| Woodcraft Supply Corp.<br>313 Montvale Avenue<br>Woburn, Massachusetts 01801 | Usual woods, glues, hand and power tools, abrasives, finishes | Catalog 50¢ |

## MANUFACTURERS

| | | |
|---|---|---|
| American Edelstaal, Inc.<br>1 Atwood Avenue<br>Tenafly, New Jersey 07670 | Unimat power tools | Catalog |
| Dremel Manufacturing Co.<br>4915 21st Street<br>Racine, Wisconsin 53406 | Dremel power tools | Literature |
| Merit Abrasive Products, Inc.<br>201 West Manville Street<br>Compton, California 90224 | Sand-O-Flex and Grind-O-Flex abrasive wheels | |
| Stanley Tools<br>Box 1800—Advertising Services<br>New Britain, Connecticut 06050 | Hand tools | Catalog:<br>"Joy of Accomplishment" |

## ORGANIZATIONS

| | |
|---|---|
| International Wood Collectors Society<br>c/o Willard G. Cookman<br>3155 Edsel Drive<br>Trenton, Michigan 48183 | National Carvers Museum<br>14960 Woodcarver Road<br>Monument, Colorado 80132 |
| Marquetry Society of America<br>2050 Eastchester Road<br>Bronx, New York 10461 | National Woodcarvers Association<br>7424 Miami Avenue<br>Cincinnati, Ohio 45243 |

# Index

(C.S. = Color Section)

## A

Abrasive papers, 40
Afghanistan, 116, 117
African objects, 4, 6, 8, 9, 11-13, 15-17, 19, 119, 228
Allan, John R., 177, 178
Almquist, Ed, 181
Altar Head, Benin, 13
Armijo, Federico, 180
Art Nouveau, 18
Ayers, Doug, 164, 165, C.S.


## B

Baj, Enrico, 184, 185, 187
Bar, 154
Bauer, Hannah, 235
Bauer, John, 136, 200
Bauhaus, 18
Beads, 86-89
Bendon, Tom, 137, 214
Benson, Skip, 227
Bickel, John, 93, 153, 215
Blum, Rita, C.S.
Blunk, J. B., 14, 15, 131, 134, 135, 137, 138, 229
Boiger, Peter, 137, 140, 141
Bookends, 174
Bowls, 5-7, 18-21, 52-59, 62, 63, 68, 69, 96, 113, 126-35, 139, 143, 185, 200, C.S.
    turning, demonstration, 52-55
Boxes, 2, 3, 58, 63, 99, 105, 115, 147, 187, 199, 201, 225, C.S.
Boyd, Don, 142
Brazil, 17
Breadboards, 106, 136, 137, 202, 203
Brewerton, William E., 186, 188-95
Brooks, Jon, C.S.
Buckles, 178, 185
Bump, Daniel B., 236, 237
Bump, Deborah D., 234, 236, 237
Butter dish, 143
Buttons, 177


## C

Cabinets
    goblet, 226
    jewelry, 225
    radio, 215
    ring display, 226
    telephone, 216, 217
    wall, 200
Candle holder, 93
Canes, 168, 169
Capri Taurus, 231, C.S.

Carbon dating, 4
Carey, Craig, 234
Carlin, David, 172, 173
Carpenter, Arthur (Espenet), 20, 21, 107, 149, 152, C.S.
Carpenter, Tripp, 91
Carving, 114-83
    hand, demonstration, 122, 123
Catlett, Dick, 179
Chain saw, 126-29
Chasen, tea, Japanese, 3
Chess set, 91
Chinese bowl, 5
Chisels, 118, 120
Chocolate whip, 7
Clamps, 37
Clock, 108-12, 213-15, C.S.
Combs, 17, 157, 176
Constructing and carving, 204-37
*Craft Horizons*, 16, 20
Crematorial urns, 182, 183, C.S.
Cribbage board, 179
Cummings, Frank E., III, 16, 17, 115, 116, 144, 145, 149, 156, 157, 186
Cumpston, Robert, 93
Cutting boards, 106, 136, 137, 202, 203


## D

Dally, Ada, 91
Daniells, Bob, 155, 212, 222, 235
Davis, Hal E., 133, 150, 151
Dean, Jeffrey, C.S.
Demonstrations
    bowls, turning, 52-55
    carving, hand, 122, 123
    chain saw, 126-29
    indexing, 70, 210
    inlay, 72-75
    jar, turning, 60, 61
    laminating, 101-3
    marquetry, 189-94
    pegging, 64-71, 197, 198
    punch cup, 76-85
    vase, inlay, 72-75
Dielectric gluing, 39, 67
Door, 180
    handles, 181
    latch, 15
Dorfer, Lisa Dahilen, 125
Dreisbach, Walter C., 37
Dremel, 124
Dulcimers, 226, 230, 231, C.S.


## E

Earrings, 196

Easton, Walter, 176
Egypt, 2
Ellsworth, Tim, 23
England, 18
Epp, Paul, 22, 23
Esherick, Wharton, 20
Espenet, 20, 21, 107, 149, 152, C.S.
Evans, William Jaquith, 98-100, 105, 107, 158, 178, 186, 196-99, 224, 226, 227, C.S.

**F**

Falwell, Bob, 147
Farris, Jack, 234
Filling holes, 78
Finishing, 39
Fischman, Irving, 58
Folk art, 10
Frinier, Richard, 216, 217

**G**

Gaughan, John, 213, 214
Gavel, 179
Gluing, 34-39, 100-103
Goblets, 42, 43, C.S.
Gordon, George, 223
Gouges, 59, 118, 120
Graham, Michael, 148, C.S.
Grinding, sharpening, 48, 49, 118, 119, 121
Gumball Machine, 104

**H**

Hand tools, 22, 23, 35, 37, 59, 118-24
Hanner, Bill, 178
Hardwood, 24, 26
  chart, 41
Harris, Stephen, 23
Headpieces, African, 11, 13
Headrest, 9
Higbee, Bob, 90, 93
Hilbert, John, 174
Hogbin, Stephen, 19, 94-97, 140, 179
Hogue, Leroy, 135, 154
Holland, Harvey, 160-62, 166, C.S.
Horgos, Bill, 167, 170-73
Hunter, Bill, 160-62, 166, C.S.
Hunter, Lawrence B., 52-59, 62, 76-89, 101-3, 116, 139, 142, 147, 177, 179, 213, C.S.
Hutch, 195
Hutchinson, Milon, 58-62, 64-71, 196, 210, 211, C.S.

**I**

Indexing, 65, 71, 211
  demonstration, 70, 210
India, 9
Indian, American, 2, 3, 9

Indonesia, 3, 10, 116, 117
Inhofe, Jack, C.S.
Inlay, 184-203
Insetting, demonstration, 72-75

**J**

Japan, 8, 9, 172
Jar, turning demonstration, 60, 61
Jars, 58, 60-62, 64-68, 93, 115, 144-46
Jewelry, 196
Jewelry boxes/chests, 14, 15, 20, 21, 99, 148-54, 201, 207, 218-25, C.S.
Johnson, Jocko, 63, 126-29, 143, 146, 166, 167, 178, 186, C.S.
Johnson, S. C., Company, 16
Johnson, Stephen R., 17, 143, 157, 237
Joinery, 206-9
Joints, woodworking, 206-9
Jones, Lawrence R., 115, 159, 218, 219, 226, 230
Joss-stick holder, 14, 15

**K**

Kaplan, Charles M., 57, 99, 100, 106, 163, C.S.
Kiburi, Fundi, 151
King, Sterling, 147, 158
Knife holder, 200
Kopel, Paul, 100, 108-13
Krisel, Elisabeth, 207
Krueger, Wayne O., 235

**L**

Lacagnina, Tom, 158
Ladles, 140, 142
Laminating, 98-113
  demonstration, 101-3
  foam model, 108-12
Laske, Lyle, 132, 224
Lathe, 44-55
  drawing, 97
  spinning, 79-85
Lehman, Robert, 136
Lindquist, Mark, 57, C.S.
Lindquist, Melvin, VIII, 1, 57
Lingo, Dennis, C.S.
Lock, Dogon, 15

**M**

McCallister boxes, 148, C.S.
McQueen, Peter, 230
Magazine rack, 204
Magnifying glass, 177
Malmlund, Ann, 135, 186
Malmlund, Wilfred, 215

Marquetry, 185-201
Mask, 12
    safety, 35
Matthews, Harriett, 231
Mexico, 7
Miele, Al, 201
Miniatures, 170-73
Mirrors, 16, 17, 105, 112, 155, 159, 199, 201
Mitchell, Bruce, C.S.
Mordaunt, Mel, 43, 72-75, 92, 143, C.S.
Morinaka, Dennis, 14, 15
Morris, William, 18
Music box, 195
Musical instruments, 226-31, C.S.


N

Netsuke, 8, 9, 172
Nyiri, Joe, 114, 115


O

"Objects: U.S.A.," 16
Oceanic, 4, 6, 7, 8
Oriental, 2, 14, 15
O'Rourke, Jay, 58, 143, 176
Osgood, Jere, 139, 214, C.S.


P

Pan, Marta, 175, 181
Paraphernalia, 170-73
Pasek, Jim, 168
Paulson, Mark, 225
Pegging demonstration, 64-71, 197, 198
Pierson, Conway, 204, 205
Pinto, Edward R., 10, 14, 16
Pipe holder, 227
Pipes, 166, 167, C.S.
Plugs, 66-71
Power tools, 30-34, 44-55, 65-67, 70-77, 124,
    126-29, 210, 211
Punch cup, spinning demonstration, 76-85, C.S.
Puppet head, 3, 10
Puzzle, 175, 234, 235


Q

Quiroz, José Margaro, 122, 123


R

Raab, Wayne, 106, 224
Rack
    clothes, 114
    hat, 225
    magazine, 204

Rainbow, 177
Rich, Joel, 167, C.S.
Robin, Stephen, 153
Robinson, Trevor, 229
Ross, Hal, 223


S

Sabin, Christopher, 158, 202, 203
Safety masks, 35
Salad servers, 140, 141
Salleroli, Robert, 201
Sanding, 40, 51, 77
Sharpening, grinding, 48, 49, 118, 119, 121
Shelf unit, 180
Smith, Carol, 104
Smith, Terry Allen, 157, 180
Softwood, 24, 26
Spaulding, Patricia, 133
Speakers, 179
Spindle turning, 86-89
Spinning, metal cup, 79-85
Spinning wheel, 212
Staff, 13, 168
Stand
    flower, 205
    letter, 204
Stephens, Keith E., 58, 63, 130, 139, 185, 186,
    200, 201
Stocksdale, Bob, VIII, 20, 21, 56
Strini, Robert, 220, 221


T

Tabletops, 184-86
Taylor, Tom, 134, 185
Telephone holders, 216, 217
Tobaro, Vince, 158
Tools, 22-37, 118-24, 126-29, 210, 211
    crocheting, 176, 177
    netting, 176, 177
    spinning, 176, 177
    weaving, 176, 177
Tornheim, Norm, 182, 183, C.S.
Toro, Euripides, 92, 93, 163
Townley, Hugh, 232, 233
Toys, 232-37, C.S.
Tramel, Tom, 152
Traynor, Jim, 18, 19, 42, 43, 116, 134, 155, C.S.
Trays, 130-35, 138, 139
Treen, 10, 14, 16
Trout, Robert, 130, C.S.
Turning, 42-97
Turning, spindle, 86-89
Tuttle, Elizabeth, 159, C.S.


U

Unimat, 50, 51, 124
Utensils, 136, 142, 143, C.S.

V

Valenza, Dan L., 56, 132, 137, 138, 143, 152, 154
Vase, inlaid, demonstration, 72-75
Vases, 43, 58, 75, 91-93, C.S.


W

Wade, Bennett, 125
War club, 8, 9
Wayang golek, 3, 10
Weed vases, 90, 98, 99, 106, 160-65, 173

Welding, wood, 39, 67
Wiley, Chuck, 233
Wine decanter, 42, 43, C.S.
Wood identification, 25
    selection chart, 31
    sources, 30
    structure and physical properties, 23-31


Z

Zucca, Ed, 142